cat

D0328335

The 7 Irrefutable Rules

of
Small
Business
Growth

The 7 Irrefutable Rules

of

Small
Business
Growth

Steven S. Little

WILEY

John Wiley & Sons, Inc.

Published by John Wiley & Sons, Inc., Hoboken, New Jersey.
Published simultaneously in Canada.

For general information on our other products and services please contact our Customer Care Department within the United States at (800) 762-2974, outside the United States at (317) 572-3993 or fax (317) 572-4002.

Wiley also publishes its books in a variety of electronic formats. Some content that appears in print may not be available in electronic books. For more information about Wiley products, visit our web site at www.wiley.com.

Library of Congress Cataloging-in-Publication Data:

Little, Steven S.
  The 7 irrefutable rules of small business growth / Steven S. Little.
    p.   cm.
  Includes index.
  ISBN 0-471-70760-0 (pbk.)
  1. Small business—Management—Handbooks, manuals, etc. I. Title: The 7 irrefutable rules of small business growth. II. Title.
  HD62.7.L58   2005
  658.02′—dc22
                     2004022890

Printed in the United States of America.

10 9 8 7 6 5

*To the memory of
my nephew Dean,
who gave us all the gift of perspective this summer.*

CONTENTS

PREFACE

DID I REALLY SAY "IRREFUTABLE"?

Yea, I sure did. Ir-re-fu-ta-ble. There . . . I said it again. Without question, this is the one word that best describes what I'm trying to say. However, like many words, this one may have different meanings for different readers. To get us off on the right foot, I want to be sure that you and I are clear on *my* meaning. Let me explain.

SOME BACKGROUND

Throughout much of the 1980s and 1990s, I was president of three different fast-growth businesses. In each case, these businesses went from pretty small to considerably bigger (but still pretty small in the grand scheme of things). The biggest one reached more than $12 million in revenue and 100 employees, and all three went through significant growth phases. At a relatively early age, I did learn a few things about what it takes to grow a small business.

I also learned that I liked talking about small business growth more than I liked actually doing it. I come from a long line of teachers and orators, and eventually the pull of that familial persuader gene proved more than I could resist. I decided in early 1998 (along with my inexplicably under-standing spouse) to pursue a full-time career as an indepen-dent consultant and speaker, specializing in the area of business growth for the privately held business. So far, so good.

Soon after, people began to hire me. In almost every case, they hired me based on my experience growing smaller busi-nesses into bigger ones. That's what gave me credibility in their eyes. Whether it was as a speaker or a consultant, it was my past success that got their attention. I have now spoken di-rectly with literally tens of thousands of owners and managers of private enterprises. To this day, people still usually hire me based on my real-world experience.

But here's an interesting thing. As I said before, I did learn a few things about growing businesses while I was doing it. How-ever, I've learned much, much more about the concept of busi-ness growth since becoming a consultant, speaker, and "expert" in the field. What I've learned, combined with my experience growing small companies, is really what I bring to the table.

For years, I've immersed myself in the study of business growth. Who does it? Why do they do it? Why does this owner make it work and not that one? What do the academicians say on the subject? Successful entrepreneurs? Other self-proclaimed experts? The media? It's a fascinating subject and one in which your sources of information are never exhausted.

So what have I learned? For one thing, I've learned that back when I thought I knew everything I could on the subject of growth, I actually knew very little. I've also learned that the more I know about my chosen field, the less definitive I can be. In other words, the more I see and hear and experience what it takes to grow a privately held business, the less able I am to make sweeping pronouncements and general state-ments of truth.

For every small business study that points in a specific direction, there's invariably another that points in exactly the opposite direction. I can get consensus from one group of business owners on one idea, only to be shot down as irrelevant by the next. Even some of my own nuggets of wisdom, slowly unearthed during my many years of digging in the trenches, have proven to be nothing more than fool's gold.

But I *have* found a few concepts that seem to resonate with people in the know—people who have witnessed sustained, profitable growth. Through years of dedicated effort (aka trial and error), I've managed to hone in on a few big ideas that seem to make sense—ideas with which people I respect appear to agree.

How do I know they agree? It has more to do with what they *don't say* than what they do. On the whole, company leaders who've had even a modest amount of success become stark-raving "experts." (Believe me, as a former company president, I know.) They are never shy about shooting down anyone or anything that espouses ideas that are contrary to their own experience. (Believe me, as a speaker and consultant, I know.)

These seven rules of small business growth that I include in this book are not rules because anyone in particular agrees with them. Instead, it's because I can't find any credible individuals inclined to disagree with them. To me, that is exactly what makes them so gosh-darn *ir-re-fu-ta-ble*. It's not that they're scientifically proven. It's that no one wants to disprove them, because almost everyone already agrees with them. Does that make sense?

You'll find that I like to make use of analogies, so here goes the first of many. Everyone seems to agree that a rose is beautiful. The notion that a rose is beautiful is irrefutable, despite the fact that it would be impossible to prove. Sure, I guess we could conduct some type of poll about attitudes toward rose beauty by various demographic groups, culminating in a statistical proof of general rose beauty across the human race. No one does this, though, because it's silly. A rose is beautiful, and everyone knows it.

The rules I present here are important, and everyone "in the know" knows it. They are irrefutable.

OTHER STUFF YOU NEED TO KNOW BEFORE WE GET STARTED

This is not a checklist book. Every year, I speak to literally tens of thousands of business owners and managers interested in growth. After the event, people often call or e-mail me with additional questions. Without a doubt, the second most common question people ask me is, "What book can I buy that will tell me how to grow my business?" (By the way, the most common is, "How can I become a speaker?" That answer I'll save for another day.)

The book question is an interesting one for a couple of reasons. First, they never say "read." It's always what book should I "buy." Perhaps I'm thinking about it too much, but the question implies (to me, anyway) that the mere act of purchasing the book will somehow help your business grow. My editor estimates that 20 percent or less of all business books purchased are ever read.

Second, the idea that someone has written a book that can give you specifics on how to grow your business is ludicrous. J. Paul Getty (a pretty successful growth guy) once said, "No one can possibly achieve any real and lasting success or 'get rich' in business by being a conformist." While a guaranteed 17-point growth guide checklist would undoubtedly be popular, it would also be irresponsible. Checklists don't grow businesses.

Instead of offering a checklist, this book identifies and examines those areas in which growth organizations concentrate their efforts. It is within these areas that the real magic happens, and that magic is up to you: the innovations and the revelations, the evolutions and the revolutions, doing it differently than anyone before, executing better than anyone has before. This is the stuff of real, sustained, profitable growth. In other words, I'm not telling you what to do; I'm suggesting where you should be looking to do it. At the end of each "rules" chapter, I have listed some suggested next steps. In no way should these be taken as specific suggestions. They are merely examples of exercises and questions you might consider to help you find your unique perspective on opportunity.

This is not a financial book. Any organization, big or small, needs to build a system that is able to deliver timely and consistent information about the financial health of the organization to the people who run the organization. Every business I ever headed produced a daily one-page "morning report" that highlighted the most important data for the day, month-to-date, and year-to-date. Revenue, orders, accounts payable, accounts receivable, inventory levels, and the so-called "quick ratio" (a measure of liquidity) were just a few of the numbers we considered every day. An Income Statement, a Balance Sheet, and a Cash-Flow Statement were produced and studied every month, without exception. I strongly suggest you do the same, because it will help you grow your business.

Having said that, this is the last you'll hear about financials in this book. The truth is that for many, if not most, business owners, it's a rather dry subject. It's also a topic that has been covered very well by many others over the years. Both of these considerations had some bearing on my decision to limit its direct exposure here. However, I would maintain that financials play a critical role throughout this book, although they are not highlighted.

Finding and keeping the best and the brightest when you can't make payroll due to poor cash flow management decisions is impossible. How can you expect to better leverage the power of technology when you can't identify the problem areas on your P&L Statement? One of the most important customer-driven processes for most companies is the timely delivery of products or services. Properly managing your inventories, be it products, parts, or man-hours, is an important financial consideration with huge customer satisfaction implications linked to it.

I think you get the idea. Each of the seven rules in this book depends on your organization's ability to monitor and interpret its financial data. While you don't have to be a CPA, it really helps if you know how to keep score. As we say here in North Carolina, "'nuff said."

RULES REALLY ARE MADE TO BE BROKEN

The word *rule,* like *irrefutable,* has many meanings and connotations. Look it up in your thesaurus, and you'll find similar words such as *decree, imperative,* and *law*—pretty strong stuff. You'll also find some synonyms much closer to my meaning in this book, such as *conventional, usual,* and *customary.* For example, "In growth companies, hard work is the rule, not the exception." That's how I want you to take these so-called rules—not as laws to which you need to surrender but, instead, general courses of action that seem to work for many others.

The last impression I want to leave with anyone is that you must follow these seven rules or you will be unable to grow successfully. That's simply not the case. My intent here is to offer insights into the broad areas in which I've seen innovation and execution make a real difference in privately held companies. From these insights, it's my hope that you will discover your own new ways to realize the full potential of your business.

PROFIT IS IMPORTANT

As I travel the country speaking to groups of entrepreneurs, there's often one person at the end of my time who wants to play "stump the speaker." These are usually good-natured people who aren't trying to raise a big fuss. But they do want to see if they can trip up this "expert" with the microphone. Over the years, like a stand-up dealing with hecklers, I've heard most of the comments meant to throw me. By far the most common example is something like, "Steve, you've talked a lot today about growth. What about profit? Don't you think profit is more important than growth?"

So here's the answer I give them: an emphatic "yes" and "no."

Yes, in this sense: For those people who don't want to grow, maximizing profitability is the most important thing. Big businesses often milk their brands for profit when growth becomes too difficult or expensive. Many small business owners also have good reasons they might not want to grow. They may be happy with their current level. They may have other interests outside the business that keep them busy. They might not want employees. Whatever their reasons, they, too, look for ways to milk their business for profits. I have no problem with that stance. It's a perfectly reasonable way to go about managing your business. I caution only against the potential for undernourishment that might cause the milk to dry up sooner then anticipated.

However, for the privately held business determined to grow, profit is *not* more important than growth. In fact, you simply can't divorce one from the other. Growth cannot be achieved indefinitely without profit. Profit becomes increasingly difficult to perpetuate for any length of time without growth. Throughout this book, I use words like *sustainable* and *successful* to modify the word *growth*. When I use those words, you can assume I'm talking about *profitable* growth. Profits are a great way to measure success. Profits are often the best way to fund organic growth. Profits help us measure our performance. Profits matter, but not more than growth. Indeed, they are ultimately the same thing.

What Do I Mean When I Say "Growth?"

However you choose to measure or define growth is probably how I would measure or define it. If you decide to pursue a growth rate of 3 percent next year, then that's your definition of growth as it relates to your business. I would not try to convince you otherwise on such a personal decision. If your goal is to make the Inc. 500 list and grow over 1,000 percent over the next five years, then that's also a legitimate benchmark of growth. Either way, the rules I've presented here and the lessons I've shared from my experience will, I believe, help you. You see, I think growth is as much a mind-set as it is a fixed goal. The foundations on which you build growth are the same, regardless of the size or duration of the plan.

If you are ready to grow your business, I am confident this book will help you. If it can offer just one really solid idea that makes a significant contribution to your growth efforts, I will feel I've accomplished my goal for this book. If that happens, I hope you'll e-mail me to let me know: steve@stevenslittle.com.

ACKNOWLEDGMENTS

If you are included in this book, I sincerely and profusely thank you. Whether you are a client, an acquaintance, a vendor, a friend, or a family member, I appreciate your letting me tell your story.

There are a couple of people who aren't named in the book, but without whom this endeavor would never have made its deadline. Tim Leffel is a kindred spirit, talented freelance editor, Yucatecan neighbor, and new friend. I can only hope his wife and daughter aren't cursing my name too badly these days. Amy Little, my wife of 20 years, has been the logistics expert, fact checker, and BS detector on this project from the start. Without these two, there would be no book.

I am also in great debt to Jeffrey Gitomer for introducing me to many people, including my new editor and buddy, Matt Holt, and all the other great folks at Wiley. Tamara Hummel is one of the nicest people I've ever met and a true pleasure to work with. I can only assume that I will feel the same way about Shannon Vargo when I meet her. Based on our phone work, that will undoubtedly be the case. Her edits have significantly improved this book. Martha Mangelsdorf has also contributed immensely to this final product, with both her keen eye for style and a thorough understanding of issues surrounding small business. Thanks for working on such a tight time crunch, Martha.

Finally, I would like to say thanks to my son Tyler, who hasn't seen much of his dad the past couple of months. Let's get to Pan y Vino soon and blow Dad's diet!

ABOUT THE AUTHOR

Steven S. Little is a much sought-after writer and consultant on the subject of business growth and the future of opportunity. As Senior Consultant for *Inc.* since 1998, he speaks to thousands of owners and managers of growing organizations each year.

He also regularly speaks for some of the world's leading companies, institutions, and associations, including UPS, Sprint, Microsoft, Bank of America, Young Entrepreneurs' Organization, and chambers of commerce around the world. His style has been described as "real world," "highly credible," and "uniquely engaging." To see him in action, check out his web site at www.stevenslittle.com. You've probably never seen anything quite like it.

Through the 1980s and 1990s, Steve was president of three fast-growth companies. Both FAME, Inc. and ERB Industries achieved profitable growth rates of over 500 percent during his tenure. As president of The Queensboro Shirt Company, Steve helped to build one of the country's most successful sites for Internet commerce.

Steve began his career in advertising with Foote Cone & Belding and DKB Advertising. Steve is a graduate of Miami University and has studied at the Institute for Management Development in Lausanne, Switzerland, and The Future Studies Masters Program at the University of Houston (Clear Lake). Steve and his wife Amy and son Tyler live in both sunny Wilmington, North Carolina, and historic Mérida, Mexico.

1

A Realist's View of the Small Business Landscape

Small business success plays a vital role in this country's mythology. You know the stories: the poor immigrant with 50 cents in his pocket who goes on to run a chain of 20 restaurants, the husband and wife who toil away for years and get the one big break that makes them millionaires, the grandma who makes cookies in her kitchen and ends up running a company with hundreds of employees, and the two nerds who create a software program in their garage and then sell it to IBM for a few billion dollars.

We love these stories because they capture the American spirit. The rugged individual who triumphs against all odds is quintessentially "us." Yet, growing a company is by no means a Horatio Alger yarn, and the myths are often offset by a more sobering reality. A special small business report in the *Wall Street Journal* in 2004 led off with the following:

Last year, the U.S. gave birth to over half a million new firms. Equally telling, nearly the same number of firms closed their doors in the same period. What this means is however much we glorify and obsess over success in the workplace, the notion of failure must go hand in hand with it.

That's an important point. While there are indeed factors that make it a good time to be an entrepreneur in America, there are also factors that make it a challenging time to be running your own business. In fact, if someone asked me whether it is the best of times or the worst of times for small business in America, I could argue either point of view. In my opinion, the current state of small business could be accurately described as both the best and worst of times—and I explain why later in this chapter. But first, let's take a realistic look at what the term *small business* encompasses.

WHAT IS SMALL BUSINESS?

Is there really any such thing as small business? The term conjures up a wide range of imagery. The U.S. Small Business Administration (SBA) defines both a sole proprietorship and a firm with 499 employees—and everything in between—as being a small business. An individual selling quilts at a monthly flea market would seemingly have little in common with a 400-person software design firm. Obviously, lumping all small businesses like these together is ridiculous. In some ways, the SBA has admitted as much, in that its own definitions for what constitutes a small business run for 29 pages. (A 2004 effort to simplify the description continues.)

So here are the facts. You may think you don't need to know this to grow your business, but I encourage you to stay with me. The U.S. Census Bureau 2002 report showed that there were 22 million small businesses operating in the United States. However, look at the numbers a little more closely, and you'll quickly see that approximately 17 million of these businesses don't have any employees. Some are simply shells set up by accountants and attorneys for tax purposes. Others are enterprises that can't or don't want to get any larger than they already are. Despite not having any employees, you are probably a small business if:

- You sell candles, cleaning products, or cosmetics on a very part-time basis and make a few hundred dollars in profit per year.
- You lost your job in a corporation but got hired by the same company as an independent contractor.
- You are 70 years old and retired, but you do a little consulting on the side.
- You have a booth at local art festivals to sell your handmade crafts.
- You buy things and "flip" them for a profit: cars, rental houses, collectibles, and so on.
- You live off the income from your investment activity.

There's nothing wrong with these enterprises. They make money for somebody, so the IRS rightfully considers them more than a hobby. Some of them even give people a pretty luxurious lifestyle. But these "small businesses" seldom lead to more employees being hired, and very few of them grow beyond a one-person entity. In many cases, the person conducting the work doesn't want the business to grow. The intention is to make a living or earn a little extra spending money.

Other nonemploying firms are truly small businesses interested in growth. The following are examples of the nonemploying firms interested in growth versus the comparatively static types previously listed:

- You've worked in the same industry for a number of years, and you've recently decided to forge out on your own to build the proverbial "better mousetrap."
- You are a skilled craftsperson who hasn't needed another person yet but hopes to reach that point someday soon.
- You've been in business for quite a number of years as a sole practitioner but are now giving serious consideration to expansion.
- You've been in business only a short time but have always had a goal of growing your customer/client base.
- After years of hitting singles as a one-person business, a customer approaches you with a home-run opportunity that you can't fulfill by yourself.

For the purposes of this book, I assume that a business interested in growth either is or plans to be an employing firm. Are there examples of one-person firms that achieve growth through outsourcing and "virtual teams"? Absolutely! Technology is making this easier and easier every day. But at this point, these companies are in the distinct minority.

This book targets those who want to grow their business. Throughout, I assume that you already have a small business—probably with employees—or that you're intending to get to that point sooner rather than later. Most of the observations I make are aimed at helping you grow a business that probably has at least a handful of employees but hasn't gotten so big that it has taken on a corporate life of its own. It's in the size range of roughly 5 to 99 employees that a lot of the important growth milestones take place in a company's development. However, these numbers are rather arbitrary and are used primarily because the government divides up segments of data at these points. If your business is smaller than five employees—but you're trying to grow—you'll also find just as many good insights and ideas that will help you get to the next level.

Understand, however, that it is the fast-growing companies that really create job growth. The Ewing Marion Kauffman Foundation, which promotes entrepreneurship in America, notes: "New fast-growth companies comprise around 350,000 firms out of a total of six million U.S. businesses with employees. Yet, this small base of companies created two-thirds of net new jobs in the 1990s."

The Small Firm

If you have at least one employee, you have made a first dramatic step toward growth. That first hire changes everything. It changes your division of labor, day-to-day responsibilities, productivity, cost structure, and tax status. Firms with even one full-time employee have more in common with those who have a handful than they do with most nonemploying firms.

In 2001, there were more than 3.4 million firms that paid some payroll but had four or fewer employees. More than 5.5 million people work for these firms. Granted, some of the companies are undoubtedly cases of a nonperforming family member being paid for tax purposes, but this is a huge group nonetheless. The category represents over 60 percent of the employing firms in this country. It also represents the wellspring from which many fast-growth companies emerge.

The 5- to 99-Employee Firm

This is the category that most big business marketers think of when they are targeting "small business." More than 2 million companies fit into this category, employing more than 35 million Americans. This is where you find the emerging growth companies. It is here where the first big leaps in growth occur: moving from a half-million dollars in revenue to $2 million, from $2 million to $10 million. Every year, *Inc.* honors the 500 fastest growing, privately held companies in this country. The majority of these Inc 500 firms fall within this category.

Don't get me wrong; a lot of companies in this category do not fit my definition of *growing*. A significant portion are indeed declining. However, it is within this category that I usually find the most current and compelling ideas on growth.

The 100- to 499-Employee Firm

To have reached this level, firms in this category have already experienced at least one period of significant growth. Almost no one does a start-up with 100 or more employees. According to the SBA, in 2001 there were more than 85,000 businesses in this category. While they represent less than 2 percent of all employing firms, more than 16 million people work in companies this size.

MOST MISLEADING SMALL BUSINESS MYTHS

As mentioned before, I can argue that this is both the best and worst of times for small business in America. Whenever I tell people I have good news and bad news, they want to hear the bad news first to get it out of the way. I know that I risk losing your enthusiasm (and believe me, you're going to need plenty of that) by starting this book on a cautionary note. None of us can succeed, however, until we first acknowledge the difficulties inherent in managing a private enterprise. Despite what most politicians and many people in the general public think, small business success is not quite as easy as some would have us believe. As a serial entrepreneur buddy of mine says, "It's gotten real easy to start a new business. Everybody wants to help you now. The problem is, it's getting harder than ever to actually make a buck at it." Seventy-two percent of respondents to a May 2004 *Inc.* poll agreed: "Entrepreneurship is getting harder."

The following positive myths about entrepreneurship are repeated so often, and in so many ways, that many people accept them as facts.

Myth 1: Business Owners Have More Independence

If you are a small business owner, especially one with a family, you know what a joke this myth is. The small business owner that Hollywood portrays is talking on her cell phone from the beach house, golfing with his buddies in the afternoon, or attending social functions during his many free evenings. She has loads of time to go to the kids' ballgames and recitals or take leisurely vacations. It's a nice life indeed. Those workaholics who neglect their spouses and kids or spend late nights at the office don't own their own company—they work for heartless corporations.

We know this portrayal is not true. According to the 2003 Inc. 500 survey, nearly a third of these fast-growth company heads work more than 60 hours a week.

Running alongside this notion of personal independence is the idea, "Finally, I'll be my own boss." For many, this is one of the primary reasons they start a small business. They've had it with being told what to do. But as most business owners soon discover, they've simply traded one boss for a whole host of other bosses. The simple act of incorporation calls for properly dotted i's and crossed t's in triplicate. Whether the lender is your brother or your banker, once you borrow money, you've created a potential supervisor. The state and federal revenue services demand quarterly reports just like any manager.

Once you hire your first employee, you've really got someone to answer to. Employees are funny. They expect you to perform a variety of functions especially for them. They assume that their problems outweigh any you may have. They consistently second-guess your decisions. They expect you to be there when they arrive and still be there when they leave. Sounds just like a boss to me!

One big difference, though: These bosses expect you to pay *them* for their efforts, whether you have the money in your account or not.

Please understand this. I am far from being anti-employee. Chapter 8 is devoted entirely to the importance of people in your organization, and it's the primary theme throughout the book. I'm simply trying to point out how taxing all of these new overseers can be. It's one of the biggest surprises for the emerging growth business owner. Consider yourself forewarned.

Myth 2: Business Owners Make a Lot of Money

If you are a small business owner already, this one doesn't need much of an explanation. Many wannabe entrepreneurs fantasize about leaving the confines of working for someone else. They think starting their own company will make them wealthier than being an employee. In some cases it is true, but on the whole, it is not.

According to the National Federation of Independent Business (NFIB), the average business owner makes between $40,000 and $50,000 per year. That's not terrible—it pays the bills—but a lot of skilled people could make that amount or more working for someone else with a lot less risk and fewer hours.

For a *growing* small company, however, the rewards can indeed be great. Among the Inc. 500 class of 2003, 78 percent reported a net worth of over $1 million. Nearly half were multimillionaires. One in five was worth more than $7.5 million. Keep in mind that these are the elite, however. The median five-year growth rate of these 500 companies was a whopping 692 percent.

The lesson from these statistics is this: Running a business that is surviving will make you a living, but perhaps less than you would make working a salaried job with someone else's company. Run a company that is growing rapidly, however, and there is serious money to be made. The distinction is in the pace of growth.

In 1996, authors Thomas J. Stanley and William D. Danko published their landmark book, *The Millionaire Next Door* (Marietta, GA: Longstreet Press, 1996). Their 258 page book has much to say about the wealthiest people in our country. The quick, one-line synopsis most people remember from this book is that most millionaires work in unassuming, everyday endeavors. In other words, they are, on the whole, welding contractors and pest controllers, not investment bankers and trust fund recipients. To many, including me, this was a fascinating revelation. It also helped fuel an ever-growing fire of enthusiasm for entrepreneurship.

It is also important, however, to fully understand the authors' findings. It is true that more than two-thirds of the millionaires in this country can be described as self-employed. The authors' research makes that very clear. However, it does not follow to say that the self-employed are most likely millionaires; far from it. While this book was written several years ago, the misconceptions some people took away from it still permeate public consciousness.

Myth 3: Business Owners Are Funded by Venture Capital and Angel Investors

The National Commission on Entrepreneurship sums up this myth nicely in its 2001 report, *Five Myths About Entrepreneurs:* "Of all the myths and misunderstandings surrounding entrepreneurship, the role of venture capital is perhaps the most exaggerated." Venture capital and money from "angel" investors flowed like water in the middle and late 1990s, but most of it went to high-risk/high-potential-reward invest-ments in tech companies, especially on the West Coast. According to the Commission, "In 1999, California received slightly more than 43 percent of all new venture capital invest-ment—a whopping $20.8 billion. Of this total, nearly $17 bil-lion was invested in Northern California."

There were more than 600 venture capital firms chasing the next big thing in the year 2000. Once the tech boom busted, the firms and money flows went with it. At the end of 2003, the surviving venture capital firms (down to fewer than 200) were sitting on about $84 billion in capital, but at least half of that was estimated to be earmarked for second-round and third-round funding of existing obligations. Only $18.2 bil-lion was actually distributed to companies. Even though the funds were flush with cash, they were still being very picky about where they put it.

What happens to the lucky souls who do manage to score venture capital funding? It's not always a gift from Santa Claus. Owners, who have staked their life savings and reputa-tion on a business, often end up giving up majority owner-ship and control. In some cases, they get pushed out of their own company.

There is a commonly held legend of the company that gets outside funding and makes its founders rich. The team then takes the company public in an initial public offering (IPO), and everyone gets even richer. Sure, it has happened now and then, especially during the height of the dot-com bubble, but those fairy tale endings represent a small sliver of the entre-preneurial world. That's not to say you'll never need, want, or receive venture capital; I just wouldn't count on it. Among the 2003 Inc 500, only 12 percent had received any venture capital funding since start-up. Only 17 percent had raised private eq-uity at any point since they began.

So where does small business financing come from? If you are running a company yourself, you probably know: maxing out credit cards, arm-twisting friends and relatives, draining the nest egg, leveraging the house, or, in many cases, all of the preceding. For most small business owners, financing is far less romantic than the magazine cover stories would have us believe.

Even companies that are successful today generally started out with relatively little capital. Among the Inc. 500 class of 2003 winners mentioned earlier, 61 percent had start-up capital of $50,000 or less. Of those, more than half had less than $20,000.

If your dreams have been spurred by the dot-com era stories of a venture-funded Ferrari, decadent parties, and company outings to Tahiti, let them go. Most private companies are funded by whatever the owners can scrape together.

Myth 4: Small Business Creates "All the New Jobs"

If you say something enough times, people start to believe it without questioning the underlying logic. Bad statistics get thrown out in some publication and, after being repeated enough times, become unquestioned facts. One of the best examples is the idea that small businesses create almost all the new jobs in America.

Politicians have done more than their part to perpetuate this myth. Pull up any politician's talking points on small business, and you're bound to see the assertion that small business creates all or most of the new jobs in the United States (see "The Little Engine That Could"). I recently attended a small business summit in Washington where in one single morning, various speakers told the audience that small business created "over half," "70 percent," "80 percent," and "over 85 percent" of all new jobs in this country.

The Little Engine That Could

Small business is the engine of economic growth in the United States.

—Vice President Al Gore, 2000

On a daily basis, small businesses demonstrate they are the economic engine that drives our economy. When big businesses are struggling and laying off workers, new small businesses have started up while established small firms have grown.

—Senator Olympia J. Snowe, 2003

Small business is the engine that drives our nation's economy, representing 97 percent of all businesses and responsible for 75 percent of new jobs created in the U.S.

—Representative Jim Moran, 2004

Seventy percent of new jobs are created by small business owners.

—President George W. Bush, 2004

[Small business] is the engine that drives our economy and provides most of the nation's job opportunities.

—Senator Kit Bond, 1997

Small businesses provide some 70 to 80 percent of jobs in America.

—Senator Arlen Specter, 2004

The small business community is the major generator of jobs in America, has been for the last 12 years.

—President Bill Clinton, 1993

(Continued)

Employment experts agree that the primary fountainhead of jobs in America is small business. We read daily of large corporations handing out thousands of pink slips, but small business entrepreneurs continue to combine their time and talent with capital and guts—and the result is jobs.

—Doug French, Nevada Policy Research Institute

Small business owners are the engine that drives the U.S. economy. They create 75 percent of the new jobs in this country.

—Maura Donahue, chair, U.S. Chamber of Commerce Small Business Advisory Council, 2004

Small businesses are the primary engine for job creation in America.

—Treasury Secretary John Snow, 2003

Small business employers are responsible for the majority of new jobs created in this country.

—Labor Secretary Elaine L. Chao, 2003

Large corporations shed jobs and wreak havoc during times of recession. On the other hand, small businesses are the backbone of our economy; they create 75 percent of all new jobs.

—Representative Nydia Velazquez, 2003

Three-quarters of the net new jobs from 1990 to 1995 were created by small businesses. They are the engine of our nation's economy.

—Representative Ed Bryant, 2003

Small businesses are the engine of the American economy. They create 75 percent of all new jobs

—JohnKerry.com, 2004

The job creation controversy has been raging for years in political and economic circles. I have tried very hard to understand the core arguments made by both sides. To better understand, I have read and listened to and e-mailed many people on the subject. After months of dedicated study, I have discovered that most government officials, economists, and other scholarly experts subscribe to two basic schools of thought as it relates to small business and job creation:

1. Small business creates practically all of the new jobs in this country.
2. Small business creates practically none of the new jobs in this country.

My concern is simply this: The more we hear about small business job creation, the more positive the spin seems to become. I don't have any specific studies that point to it, but I know the average person in this country believes that small business in general is booming. I'll have to admit, when I started this book, I believed this was true. However, when I started looking for the employment numbers to prove it, I slowly discovered a more sobering truth.

I looked very closely at the most recent Bureau of Labor Statistics numbers for small business (1990 through 2001). These are the same statistics the SBA uses for many of its research efforts. I discovered that, while the overall economy has grown and small business has grown with it, the growth has not been proportional. For example, in that 11-year period, the percentage of people in this country who work for businesses with more than zero but fewer than 99 employees fell by more than 8 percent. The payroll generated by this category as compared to total U.S. payroll also fell by more than 10 percent. At the same time, the number of people working for businesses with more than 500 employees grew by more than 7 percent, and payroll for the category grew by more than 6 percent. That didn't make any sense. Everybody knows that small business drives this economy. I became confused and did a little historical research.

In the early 1990s, Nobel-prize-winning economist Milton Friedman (one of the few economists most of us have ever heard of) wrote an article for the *Journal of Economic Literature* titled, "Do Old Fallacies Ever Die?" Friedman presented strong evidence that small businesses' job-creating potency is one of the most durable falsehoods of America's economic politics. Nonetheless, the SBA continued to release studies and reports pointing to the strength of job creation by small business. "Small Business Job Generation: From Revolutionary Idea to Proven Fact" was a typical title of the agency's research. By the end of the 1990s, the story became, in the immortal words of Lewis Carroll, "curiouser and curiouser." University of Chicago's wunderkind Dr. Steven Davis continued to find the opposite to be true. His work concluded that the job-creating prowess of small businesses rests on misleading interpretations of the data. In 1999, former SBA economist David Hirschberg published *The Job-Generation Controversy: The Economic Myth of Small Business* (Armonk, NY: M. E. Sharpe, 1999). Describing himself as a "whistle-blower," Hirschberg tried to explode this myth that small business creates most of the jobs.

What's going on here? It's complicated but, in the simplest terms, I have determined that:

- You shouldn't divorce job creation data from job destruction data.
- You can't define small business job creation unless you can define small business in general.

- Everybody is right and everybody is wrong on the job creation myth. Few tell the whole story.
- There are lies, damnable lies, and small business statistics.

So why does any of this matter to you, a person trying to grow a business? I am concerned that popular opinion has been overly influenced by rosy job-creation assertions. When politicians or the popular media get hold of these figures, it's tempting to portray small business ownership as an easy path to success. It's not. Ask anyone who has done it. There's absolutely nothing easy about it. Don't be lulled into a false sense of security by misleading statistics that refuse to die.

Myth 5: *Slow and Lumbering Big Business Is Vulnerable to Quick and Agile Small Business*

There are some good reasons this myth exists. Yes, big companies can be slow to react to new opportunities and have their areas of weakness. In General Electric's 1999 annual report, then CEO Jack Welch said, "For 20 years, we've been driving to get the soul of a small company into this sometimes muscle-bound, big-company body . . ." But we can't ignore the powerful sticks big companies wield. They can fight with deep pockets, proprietary research, and what I call "the three power L's": lobbying, litigation, and legacy. Thanks to their large campaign contributions and well-funded advocacy groups, big business has the ear of government at the federal, state, and local levels. Have you ever been done wrong by one of the big boys? Good luck collecting any money using the court system. Through legal maneuvering and abundant resources, big business can keep your case file open long beyond your financial ability to see it through. There's also something to be said for status quo, reputation, and years of community goodwill. Like most bureaucracies and institutions, big businesses are self-perpetuating. In some ways, they are similar to a medieval castle. The longer they have been around, the stronger their defenses seem to get.

Big business can marshal an army of people to quell any perceived challenges. Roughly half of all Americans work for companies employing more than 500 people. Wal-Mart alone employs approximately 1.5 million people—about equal to the entire populations of Wyoming, Vermont, and Washington, DC, combined. General Electric and Ford both employee over 300,000 people, which would make for a medium-size city. Those numbers don't even count the thousands of jobs that have been outsourced or transferred to suppliers.

And the big keep getting bigger. Las Vegas is one of the fastest growing cities in the United States, and it has one of the lowest unemployment rates. Is this because there are lots of energetic entrepreneurs starting new companies? Is it because of hundreds of private enterprises needing new people? Not exactly. When MGM Mirage and Mandalay Bay merged in 2004, the combined company employed 64,000 people. That's a lot of zeros for one city. It would take 16,000 four-person firms to employ as many people as this one casino and hotel chain.

As a speaker, I tend to spend a lot of time in just a few metropolitan areas. Las Vegas is one of them. I've spoken at local small business events in Las Vegas on many occasions over the years. The gaming industry directly affects business owners whether they are building new homes miles from the strip or running a small chain of convenience stores. When the big business gaming industry gets a cough, these guys all come down with something.

Seattle, Washington, is rightly known as a hotbed of innovative entrepreneurism. But anyone who lives there knows that Boeing and Microsoft are the thermometer by which community business health is measured.

In any of the small businesses I personally managed, concerns about what "the big guys" would do consistently kept me up at night. I worried about their chances for setting their sights on my little corner of what they might perceive to be "their market." I was equally concerned about what these lumbering giants would do accidentally. As the old saying goes, "When the elephants dance, it's the ants that get crushed." I always knew my competitive advantage against these larger players, but I also recognized how formidable a threat they could be. I never underestimated them.

THE FOUR MOST ENCOURAGING SIGNS FOR SMALL BUSINESS OWNERS INTERESTED IN GROWTH

I promised some good news about why this could be seen as the best of times for small business, so here we go. To counter the myths, I call them the four most encouraging signs.

Encouraging Sign 1: It's Cool to Be an Entrepreneur

Throughout the history of industry and commerce, positive impressions of entrepreneurs were much more rare than they are today. Little old ladies didn't brag about their granddaughter or grandson the entrepreneur until very recently. Who knows exactly how or why this shift happened. Perhaps the Reagan revolution of the early 1980s, with its emphasis on free enterprise and the power of the individual, started the trend. I tend to think the trend pushed the revolution. Certainly the disruption caused by the shift from a manufacturing focus to an information focus brought on a new type of business leader. Suddenly, nascent start-ups by unlikely characters such as Jobs and Wozniak could strike legitimate blows against giant enemies such as IBM. Whatever the cause, being an entrepreneur became cool, and the cachet has increased over the past two decades.

When spreading the good news of small business, I often tell audiences that entrepreneurs are now like rock stars. Think about it—successful entrepreneurs have become household names: Gates, Turner, Branson, Trump, Dell, Bezos. Even outside the business community, these names are well known. Successful entrepreneurs are admired and adored. People flock to hear them speak at events. We know when they get married or divorced, and the paparazzi even hound them.

Maybe the local growth business owner doesn't have the paparazzi following him or her around, but you probably know who the stars are in your community. They are featured in the local business press and held up as examples to which we should aspire. If you have any success at all in your business, regardless of your size, you can count on a steady stream of requests for interviews from journalists, photographers, and "experts" like me who are writing books. Who would have ever guessed that an entrepreneur like Donald Trump would host the number one television show in America? Frankly, I think Trump's ego-driven style and dog-eat-dog message has done as much harm as good for the small business community, but that's not my point. The point is: It's nothing short of incredible that the American public is so enthralled by the notion of entrepreneurism.

Not only have business owners become more like rock stars, but rock stars have become more like entrepreneurs. We read as much about Madonna's prowess as a "savvy business person," as we do about her music. Teenagers know as much about Sean "Puffy" Combs' (aka P. Diddy's) net worth as they do about his rhymes. The business press continually highlights the acumen of rock stars such as Bruce Springsteen, Mick Jagger, and Bono. In 2004 alone, *Inc.* featured burgeoning entrepreneur Jon Bon Jovi and rap music mogul Russell Simmons on its cover. Fascinating. Somehow I can't imagine Buddy Holly or Jimi Hendrix aspiring to be on the cover of any business publication.

Encouraging Sign 2: Banks Are Increasingly Small Business Friendly

A few decades ago, it wasn't easy to get a small business loan from a bank. Banks held all the leverage, and you would never go to one of "the big guys" to fund your business. Only the relatively small, local banks took the time to go after your market. According to a Federal Reserve study from 1996, small banks (under $1 billion in assets) lent nearly two-thirds of the money small business owners used to capitalize their companies.

However, in recent years, competition among banks has increased. Small banks still target small business, but big banks have gotten in on the game as well. According to MSNBC, from just October 2003 through July 2004, Bank of America, the largest lender to small business in the United States, reported over 10,000 new small business loans, for a total of $372.9 million.

Perhaps the big banks have figured out that some entrepreneurs end up being downright wealthy. Small business can be a great entrée into the world of high net worth individuals. Or the person's business goes from generating $100,000 per year to generating $10 million per year. If the bank can gain that business early, they know it might lead to bigger things down the line.

It has also gotten easier for banks to analyze and quantify the risks. Scoring methods changed the entire credit industry by making it easier for lenders to match rates to credit risk for things such as a car or home. In the late 1990s, big banks started using standardized scoring systems that also decreased the risk for small business loans. This allows banks to bundle loans and sell them to investors on the secondary market.

According to an SBA report in 2002, commercial banks supplied 57 percent of all credit outstanding to small business, with an overall loan balance of $484 billion. The percentage is not much lower for the fastest growing companies either: Among the Inc. 500 of 2003, half looked to banks for more capital.

The preceding reports do not automatically mean the big banks are the best ones to work with. As the SBA's state-by-state reports (at www.sba.gov/advo/stats/lending) point out, many state and regional banks work very hard to meet the needs of small business and are still tops in total dollars loaned to owners in specific areas. I can also attest to the dedication of a big bank like Bank of America, as I have spoken on their behalf around the country on many occasions. The bottom line is: There is more competition than ever for small business's banking dollars, which is certainly a net positive overall. The days when you had to go into a bank with your head down, hat in hand, asking for a loan are over—provided you have done your homework.

In August 2004, the NFIB found that "only 6 percent of small business owners reported difficulty in obtaining financing." The banks want your business. Once you show evidence of profitable growth, it won't be difficult to get their attention.

Encouraging Sign 3: The Government Increasingly Loves Small Business

Whether you look at funding, manpower, or legislative attention, the government loves small business. As "The Little Engine That Could" quotes highlighted earlier, every politician wants to at least appear to be on the small business owner's side. The Ewing Marion Kaufmann Foundation even publishes a detailed advice booklet for would-be political candidates, titled *Entrepreneurship, a Candidate's Guide.*

The U.S. government began to level the playing field for all businesses beginning in the 1930s, when the Securities and Exchange Commission was formed. The key development for small business was the founding of the SBA in 1953. In the late 1950s, the SBA introduced Small Business Investment Companies (SBICs), which started banks down the path of loaning more money to small enterprises. Now the agency's role has grown to include education, funding of research studies, and assistance in procuring government contracts. However, the SBA is still best known for the guaranteeing of small business loans, allowing banks to lend more while carrying less risk. As a result, the agency has become the largest single financial backer of U.S. businesses in the nation.

In addition, the agency helps support a whole infrastructure of 1,100 small business development centers (SBDCs) located in multiple cities in every state. These centers provide advice and education for those looking to start or grow their own business. In 2003 alone, they counseled and trained more than 687,000 clients. These days, many people wonder whether their tax dollars are being put to good use. I am regularly exposed to the work of these business development centers, and I'm here to tell you that these people really know what they are doing. If you haven't contacted your local SBDC, I suggest you do so.

The SBA is just one section of the government that loves business owners, however. Nearly every major government department, from the Department of Labor to the General Services Administration, has a staff devoted just to small business.

The NFIB is the largest advocacy organization representing small and independent businesses in Washington, DC, and all

50 state capitals. The NFIB is not funded by the government but instead wields powerful influence over decisions the government makes at every level. There are also literally thousands of trade associations, from all areas and industries, that lobby government on behalf of small business.

Besides all of these groups working to help business owners, many state and local governments have their own economic development group. Sometimes it's the chamber of commerce, an economic development agency, or something else entirely. For example, I've spoken at three events for Senator Bob Bennett of Utah, who led time management products company Franklin International Institute Inc. (now known as FranklinCovey) into the Inc. 500. He holds annual education conferences for small businesses in Utah and sits on the U.S. Senate's small business committee. The Council for Economic Development (CED), in the Research Triangle area of North Carolina, claims to be "the largest entrepreneurial support organization in the nation." While the council is primarily funded by private sources, it does receive some grants from state development coffers and coordinates programs with the state.

In many cases, local governments cooperate with state governments in trying to incubate organic growth in a specific industry. The St. Louis Chamber Regional Growth Center set up the BioBelt organization to market the area as an agricultural biotech center and attract start-ups to the region. The agency estimates that 390 plant and life sciences enterprises now call this area home and collectively employ 22,000 people. The Biotech Council of New Jersey has similar goals for its state but is focused on leveraging its existing foundation within the pharmaceutical industry.

Government increasingly loves small business, and I don't see that changing any time soon. The trend certainly isn't going to be hurt by the fact that business owners are becoming more active in politics. As I write this, for the first time in history, the leader of our nation (George W. Bush), the leader of the most populated state (Arnold Schwarzenegger), and the leader of the most populated city (Michael Bloomberg) have all been successful business owners. Before being elected to their current offices, they all spent far more time running their own enterprises than they did in politics.

Encouraging Sign 4: The Playing Field Is More Level

Earlier in this chapter I said that big business is not completely vulnerable and that the strength of big companies should be respected. However, the classic business school terms such as *sustainable competitive advantage* and *barriers to entry* are becoming more and more antiquated. As our economy moves away from a manufacturing base to being more service and information based, the traditional advantages inherent in big business have lessened.

Due in part to both technology and changing business practices, it is increasingly easier for a new company to enter an industry and easier for companies to hop across previously well-drawn territory lines. Just look at what has happened in the telecom world. Nearly every major player is struggling to make a profit, while upstarts are stealing market share with prepaid cell phones or voice-over-IP services. The airline industry faces similar struggles. The traditional legacy airlines such as United and USAir are getting hammered by the likes of recent entries JetBlue and Frontier.

Huge companies used to enjoy the advantages inherent in economies of scale. They produced and sold such a large number of items that they could effectively dissuade upstart competition. Now many consumer product companies are not even making their own products; start-ups can book business with the same contract manufacturers the big boys are using. In addition, consumers are demanding a more customized experience, whether buying a product or a service. A nimble company can sometimes keep up with trends more easily and react faster to demand.

Giant marketing budgets also created a huge advantage, and this still keeps consumer product companies such as Anheuser-Busch and Procter & Gamble on top. However, the 30-second TV spot does not have the impact it used to (partly thanks to a start-up named TiVo), and many smaller players have grabbed market share by using their limited marketing and sales promotion budgets in a more direct fashion. In some cases, good public relations, viral Web campaigns, and search engine ads have vaulted no-name companies and brands into the mainstream seemingly overnight.

Technology has also leveled the playing field for small business. As we see in Chapter 7, software, hardware, and telecommunication solutions now give small business much of the same firepower as big business. In 1990, as president of a small but growing manufacturing company, I looked into buying salesforce automation software. The price of this mid-range solution was $30,000 before training and annual support costs. Today, you and I can buy a far superior package at the local office supply retailer for around $300 (before rebate).

OUR WORLD IS CHANGING; CHANGE CREATES OPPORTUNITY

This is but the first chapter of this book. In the last chapter (Chapter 9), I go into far greater detail about the role that change will play in our future. But here's a quick preview of what I think about change. Change always represents both opportunities and threats to the status quo. Of the 500 companies making up the S&P 500 in 1957, only 74 were still on the list in 1997. That means that more than 400 companies grew and took their place. Creation and destruction are inevitable results of our economic system.

Allow me to end this chapter on this note: despite my less-than-rosy depiction of the state of small business in the first half of this chapter, I want to clearly state for the record that I am a net optimist. I believe that despite all the potential obstacles, small business will be healthier, wealthier, and larger 20 years from now than it is today. Just as the power of the individual continues to rise in our society, so, too, will the power of the businesses individuals create. I don't see anything stopping that relentless momentum.

2

ARE YOU REALLY THE ENTREPRENEURIAL TYPE?

For years now, researchers have been trying to find an "entrepreneurial" type. Can success as a business owner be predicted based on personality? How do successful business owners differ from business owners who are not successful? How do business owners differ from corporate managers? Are successful growth entrepreneurs born or developed? In many ways, this all harkens back to the whole "nature versus nurture" argument, fiercely debated by philosophers and scientists alike for a few hundred years now.

It has been my experience that independent business owners like you, when presented with information regarding anything having to do with psychological testing, fall into two distinct camps:

1. Those who find this stuff of great interest
2. Those who think it's all a bunch of BS

There are usually not too many of you who straddle the fence on this. Business owners either find psychological profiling a tremendous tool for understanding themselves and their employees, or they see it as useless quackery, analogous to horoscopes and palm readings.

In the interest of full disclosure, I think it's important to get one fact out right away: I fall into the former category. That is to say, on the whole, I think this stuff is pretty interesting and may even be useful for the business owner to know more about. However, I can't say anything for sure on the subject. I'm not enough of an expert to discern good psychological research from bad. I couldn't tell you the difference between Freudians and Jungians. I'm a "business growth" expert, not a "business personality" expert. But that didn't stop me from diving headfirst into the seemingly bottomless pit of historical perspective and academic research on the subject.

Admittedly, these scholarly findings about entrepreneurial personality can be somewhat dry. With that in mind, I've placed a synopsis of the ongoing academic debate in the appendix found in the back of this book. If you are like me and find this stuff of interest, I encourage you to read through it.

For the rest of you, here is a more concrete profile of the growth entrepreneur. It is based less on research and more on observation. In other words, despite the lack of consensus among academicians, I believe there truly are important characteristics that define the difference between entrepreneurs and growth entrepreneurs, between business owner and business builder.

Because the bulk of these characteristics come from my own observations, they are, by necessity, more subjective. However, I am confident that they will also be helpful and meaningful to readers like you.

A BRIEF HISTORY

Given the current status of entrepreneurs as rock stars in our public consciousness, it may be difficult for many to imagine that entrepreneurs have not always been held in such high regard. Aristotle and other Greek writers saw the merchant class as beneficiaries of a zero-sum environment—if an individual gained, it was at the expense of another. Indeed, even successful merchants were denied citizenship during the Greek empire's heyday. Throughout the Middle Ages, religious institutions and monarchies were disdainful toward entrepreneurs, which makes sense considering that the businesspeople created competition. Wealth creation was often viewed as an evil thing.

It wasn't until the French and English economists in the mid-eighteenth century that the economic activity of the entrepreneur was given much respect at all. The old attitudes were difficult to shake, however. Dickens's Ebenezer Scrooge character is indicative of how the successful small business owner was often portrayed.

American entrepreneurs have been categorized to fit a stereotypical profile. Ben Franklin imagined an entire country made up of shopkeepers and craftsmen, small business owners he called the "middling people." An image of the highly independent, financially motivated, winner-take-all entrepreneur came in with the Industrial Age and was reflected in movies and literature throughout the first half of the twentieth century. From *The Great Gatsby* to *Citizen Kane,* the idea of the driven, but tragically flawed, entrepreneur was enduring.

By the 1950s, some research and plenty of observational evidence led many to characterize entrepreneurs as high risk-takers and gamblers. With American corporations booming and high-paying jobs plentiful, it was seen as almost foolhardy to risk one's own money, when financial security seemed relatively ensured through lifetime employment. Remember, coming out of World War II, the United States represented over half of the world's output of goods and services.

Since the 1960s, attempts to quantify and qualify the quintessential personality type of the entrepreneur have played an important role in small business research. Like much of the academic work on small business, the results are less than conclusive but interesting and potentially telling nonetheless. But while we wait on the researchers to make up their minds, I've taken this opportunity to outline for you what I consider to be the most important traits a growth entrepreneur needs in today's increasingly complex economy.

THE 10 I'S OF EFFECTIVE
GROWTH ENTREPRENEURS

Over the past couple of decades, I have met with, worked with, worked for, and studied literally thousands of business owners who have achieved sustained periods of growth. To try to characterize them as all the same would be both irresponsible and inaccurate. Obviously, just as no two people or two businesses are alike, all growth entrepreneurs are unique. However, I have noticed uncanny similarities between those that flourish and those that flounder. Sometimes these similarities are seemingly small and insignificant. In other cases, the common trait gets to the very core of what brings their success.

I have distilled what I consider to be the essential attributes that you need to know. By no means am I suggesting that you need to exhibit all of these characteristics to be a success. In fact, there is no such thing as the perfect entrepreneur embodying all 10 of these qualities. Understand that each of the 10 I's listed is both prevalent and important. Only you can determine how important and how prevalent they are for you and your business.

1. Industrious

I have yet to meet a successful growth entrepreneur who is afraid of hard work. That's not to say that these same business all-stars are workaholics. In fact, the best growth leaders normally have very balanced lives. But when circumstances dictate, they have the intestinal fortitude to keep going as long as it takes.

The word *industrious* means hard working, but it also connotes getting something accomplished. I know many business owners who seem to be running in place. No one doubts their effort, but the results are in question. To me, industrious also means being diligent, vigorous, and committed. Entrepreneurs are task oriented, and they pursue their desired result with steely determination.

2. Interconnected

If you want to grow a business today, you can't go it alone. The complexity of managing a rapidly growing firm has simply become too potentially overwhelming for an individual. Business owners need access to experts and problem solvers. By necessity, entrepreneurs are great networkers. Many entrepreneurs are introverts (shy, energized by ideas and impressions, preferring to work alone). However, the majority come across as extraverts (outgoing, energized by people and action, preferring to work in teams) to the outside world.

Regardless of an entrepreneur's predisposition, he or she is able to balance introversion and extraversion to further the cause of the business. In this sense, entrepreneurs are like chameleons, able to change their color in varying environments. It has been my experience that they are not acting, but rather understand in their gut that to push the business forward, they have to press the flesh and be out there, visible and talkative. They do it because it has to be done.

Most growth leaders don't mind being alone, which is good because it can be lonely at the top. However, they genuinely like people and are able to get along with a wide variety of other personality types. As a result, they, too, are well liked by employees, partners, and the community at large. Are there exceptions? Sure, lots of them. But, generally, people gravitate toward a successful entrepreneur.

Interconnected also refers to entrepreneurs' tendency to flock together like birds of a feather. Organizations such as Young Entrepreneurs' Organization (YEO), Young Presidents' Organization (YPO), The Executive Committee (TEC), local and regional chambers of commerce, and industry trade groups and associations are just a few of the ways business owners share everything from best practices to life lessons.

3. Intrepid

Historically, entrepreneurs have been seen as big risk-takers. Even today, I see and hear people describe a successful entrepreneur as having "rolled the dice" or "bet the ranch." Frankly, the characterization simply isn't true. Entrepreneurs may take more financial risk than other occupations, but business owners really don't dwell on that. For them, the risk is a calculated one. Most view their efforts as highly logical, not whimsical. They have experience, knowledge, and confidence on their side, not Lady Luck.

However, I can describe entrepreneurs as being intrepid, that is to say, daring and bold. They know there is risk and uncertainty in any economic endeavor, but they aren't paralyzed by the thoughts of the downside. They see the risk as a challenge with a worthwhile reward. During a crisis, most successful entrepreneurs I know rise to a new level of courageousness.

4. Irreverent

As a professional speaker, I spend an inordinate amount of time at conferences, conventions, and business meetings. Invariably, that means lines—lines to get your badge, lines to check in at the hotel, lines to get your rubber chicken. But the worst line of all is the one for the taxi, especially when every attendee is trying to go to the same place at the same time. Taxi queues at hotels, airports, and convention centers can be a nightmare.

When I am speaking at an event where the majority of the attendees aren't entrepreneurs, people line up like well-behaved grade schoolers. They hate standing in line as much as anybody, but they assume that someone must have a system and that eventually they'll get a cab. When the meeting is dominated by entrepreneurs, however, everything changes.

To entrepreneurs, rules, systems, and policies are simply suggestions. It's not that they think they are above the rules. They really don't. But they honestly assume that if there is a line, something is seriously wrong and thank goodness they are there to fix it for everybody. When there are only one or two entrepreneurs, that attitude can be quite helpful. When there are 300, it's mayhem. I recently attended an event in Las Vegas. When the dinner hour arrived, no fewer than 50 well-intentioned business owners were actively engaged in various attempts to completely redesign the for-hire transportation system of Las Vegas. It wasn't impatience or hunger that activated their problem-solving juices. It was simply the fact that they saw something that didn't work very well and honestly thought they had a better solution, given the 10 or 15 minutes they had studied the situation.

That's what I mean by irreverent. Think of entrepreneurs as pleasant nonconformists. To them, rules aren't made to be broken, but they are negotiable. Most business founders have a long history of questioning those in authority. If the entrepreneurs like the answers, respect will follow. Give what they perceive to be an inappropriate response, and continued challenges will ensue. If the truth be known, the title of this very book plays into this widespread entrepreneurial tendency. By telling a bunch of entrepreneurs something is irrefutable, I'm banking on the assumption that most of them will spend $20 just so they can refute it!

Does this sound like you?

5. *Influential*

People often describe entrepreneurs as exhibiting high levels of leadership, but leadership means lots of different things to lots of different people.

My grandfather Stirling was one of the most outstanding leaders you could ever hope to meet. The son of a Scottish coal miner, he began working in the coal mines himself at the age of 10. As a young adult, he found himself living in the time of the Great Depression, in rural America, with little more than his superior intellect and his dreams. Over the course of the next 40 years, Thomas Stirling went on to become a respected high school football coach and later principal of a large high school in Indianapolis, Indiana. At his funeral, hundreds of former players and students came to pay their respects. For so many of these people, the word *leader* meant Thomas Stirling. However, I can assure you that my grandfather would have made a terrible entrepreneur.

What people are really referring to when they speak of leadership is an entrepreneur's uncanny ability to influence others. Most successful entrepreneurs I know are the "lead by example" type. Usually, leadership is not something entrepreneurs actively pursue. Instead, people just seem to follow them. I've heard this magnetism called everything from a cult of personality to a high-speed train that everyone wants to jump on. For the successful entrepreneur, this attraction is a natural by-product of the person's vision, enthusiasm, and proven track record. When I have observed entrepreneurs who are struggling, they are often charging just as fervently up a hill but often look over their shoulder too late to find that few, if any, have followed.

6. Ingenious

Ingenuity may be one of the most difficult qualities to describe but one of the most important for the successful growth entrepreneur to possess. Successful business owners are able to see patterns in data and events that most people cannot see. As a result, they recognize both clear opportunities and probable pitfalls long before the average businessperson. To them, growth opportunities look obvious. When they describe it to others, it sounds ingenious. You can also describe this trait as being clever, inspired, or imaginative. Either way, nearly every growth leader has it to some extent.

7. Innovative

Ingenious and *innovative* might sound very similar, and I guess they are to a certain extent. Both rely on that creative spark that eludes so many others. However, there is a clear difference between the two: Ingenuity speaks to seeing opportunities, while innovative means acting on an opportunity in a wholly original way. In other words, for Ted Turner to see that a 24-hour news channel's time had come was ingenious.

Turner's decision to announce his intentions at a cable television convention in front of thousands before telling his staff was innovative. Having veteran newsman Daniel Schorr at his side was innovative. Hiring 100 recent journalism school graduates and bringing them to Atlanta for a crash course in TV news production was innovative. See the difference?

The seven rules of growth presented in this book represent areas in which successful small business owners concentrate their efforts. In other words, it's within these seven areas that growth entrepreneurs innovate. More and more, successful entrepreneurs find compelling ways to innovate in relatively mundane companies, industries, and market segments. Look at the current list of Inc. 500 winners, and you'll find, for example, a surprising number of temp agencies, homebuilders, and restaurant chains alongside the high-tech product and service developers. Later in this book, you're going to read about a commercial printer, a pet food manufacturer, and a candle supply cataloger. While their markets may sound ordinary, I think you'll see that these companies are some of the most innovative out there.

8. Improvisational

My 13-year-old son and I have a lot in common. We look alike, we talk alike, and—sometimes to my wife's chagrin—behave alike. We also share a common penchant for comedy. We rent DVDs of stand-up comics. Our favorite television show varies but can usually be found on Comedy Central. Friends and family are amazed by our ability to recall the bits from old *Saturday Night Live* reruns.

A Bigger Challenge

Throughout this book, I use a company called PrintingForLess .com, in Livingston, Montana, as a shining example. While there are other companies featured and other ideas discussed, PrintingForLess.com pops up the most. There's a reason. In my 20-plus years of running, working with, and studying small businesses, I've yet to experience a better organization. These guys are doing it right. Their continued success is anything but dumb luck.

President and founder Andrew Field is the quintessential fast-growth entrepreneur. Born and raised in California, Field became a press operator as a young adult. That experience shaped his thinking, but he left it for other pursuits along the way. Andrew and his wife, Victoria, started a car repair facility in Livingston, Montana, in 1989. After a few years of steady but limited success, Andrew got bored. The car repair facility dealt with a fluid machinery vendor whose products intrigued Andrew. He bought the rights to distribute these products locally and grew that business into a multimillion-dollar enterprise. After a few years, the business was producing a nice income for Andrew and Victoria, but Andrew needed a greater challenge. One day while fishing with a buddy, Andrew was presented with a true challenge. The buddy was a printing press operator at an in-house printing facility. The organization was going to shut down this in-house department and the pressman was going to be out of a job.

"Hey, Andrew," the buddy said. "You know something about commercial printing. Why don't we start a commercial printing company right here in Livingston?"

That's just what they did. A few months later, in 1996, Andrew and a staff of five began their local commercial printing entity.

(Continued)

(Continued)

After a couple of years, business was doing reasonably well, but local competition was meeting his challenge, and Andrew was once again getting bored. He needed a new and bigger challenge.

In March 1999, PrintingForLess.com launched its web site. In the first couple of months, Andrew could track the number of orders received through the web site with a few checkmarks on his calendar. By March 2000, online sales had grown well beyond expectations. By 2002, PrintingForLess.com was an Inc. 500 member, with a five-year annual growth rate of over 1,000 percent. The company made the Inc. 500 list again in 2003, and I wouldn't bet against them in the years to come. From their humble six-person beginnings in 1996, the company now has more than 100 dedicated employees serving more than 30,000 customers.

As you've probably noticed, in the past few years a few shows have been built around improvisational comedy. In comedic circles, *improvisation* refers to unscripted ad-libbing where performers work in the moment, crafting comedy on the fly.

Improv, as it's called, is a natural ability that can be honed through experience. Entrepreneurs aren't necessarily funny, but they, too, rely on a sharpened ability to be in the moment and react to ever-changing cues and directions.

Most growth entrepreneurs are able to react on the fly. They never lose sight of their ultimate goal, but the route to get there can appear to change without warning to employees and outside observers. Often, this can become a point of frustration for all concerned. Entrepreneurs want to keep all their options open for as long as they possibly can. What may appear as indecisive to some is, in reality, the growth leader keeping his or her ability to improvise in play.

9. *Indefatigable*

This section of the chapter started with the trait called *industrious:* hard work, elbow grease, keeping the nose to the grindstone, leading to accomplishment. *Indefatigable* refers to a more persevering characteristic. This isn't a very well-known word, so here's a definition:

> *In-de-FAT-i-ga-ble.* Adj *maintaining a purpose in spite of counter influences, opposition, or discouragement.*

You show me a successful small business growth leader, and invariably I can show you a comeback artist. Remember those inflatable punching bag toys some of us had as a kid? For me it was a red-nosed clown with a light head and heavy bottom. No matter how hard you hit this clown, he would pop right back up. Oh, you could knock him down for a second, but he kept coming back for more. He was indefatigable. He could not be defeated. The only difference is that the clown had no brain. The indefatigable entrepreneur learns from being knocked down and is eventually able to avoid the punches (or develop a strong jaw anyway).

Not all entrepreneurs have tasted bitter defeat. Most successful growth entrepreneurs have had a mouthful. For many, their success comes not from what they did during the good times, but how they reacted when they stood at the brink of disaster.

10. *Integrity*

Over the years there have been many studies showing a high level of integrity by entrepreneurs in general. Given that these studies rely on self-reporting, I tend to put more faith in my own observations. When I look at successful entrepreneurs, I continually see that growth and integrity go hand in hand.

Perhaps because they have already reached a level of success, they are not tempted to cheat. That's certainly possible. My gut tells me, however, that growth comes in part because the leader has integrity, not vice versa.

The expression, "Cheaters never win," isn't always true if winning means money. I have met plenty of cheaters who have gotten rich. However, it has been my experience that most thriving entrepreneurs are significantly more concerned with ethics, community, and "doing the right thing" than the average citizen. I do know this: Integrity makes the road to success much easier.

MORE ALIKE THAN NOT

Business ownership among specific demographic groups has received a tremendous amount of attention in recent years. Women, minorities, senior citizens, and veterans are just a few of the groupings targeted by studies, grants, and government policies. I could undoubtedly dedicate an entire chapter to just women as business owners. However, I do not. In fact, I do not single out any specific group. Here's why.

I've read the studies, met the successful owners, listened to the experts searching for differences, and reached one overall conclusion. There really isn't much difference among growth entrepreneurs. Sure, among business owners in general, there are some differences in why they start the business, the type of business they start, their access to capital, their unique limitations to growth, and so on. The playing field isn't always as level as it should be. However, it has been my overwhelming experience that once a business owner enters the rushing waters of business growth, the differences begin to wash away. On the whole, growth entrepreneurs are much more alike than they are different. They play for the same reasons. They play with the same level of intensity. They play to win.

While I was president of growth companies, I was a member of YPO, a worldwide organization. To the casual observer, the only things this group had in common were age (everyone was under 50) and the fact that we all ran companies. My little forum of 10 business owners could not have been more diverse. However, the group immediately recognized that it was made up of nothing but kindred spirits. Age, gender, ethnicity, and religion really had no bearing on our ability to both understand and help one another.

That was nearly 20 years ago. Since that time, I've met thousands of successful entrepreneurs from all walks of life. In them I saw many of the traits I listed in this chapter, and it's those important traits that have determined their companies' unique paths, not the entrepreneurs' demographics.

3

RULE 1:
Establish and Maintain a Strong Sense of Purpose

Many people have a wrong idea of what constitutes true happiness. It is not attained through self-gratification, but through fidelity to a worthy purpose . . .

—Helen Keller

I speak to many small business owners throughout the year. Invariably, there are also a few people in the audience who think they would like to form their own company. After my presentation, many of them come up to me and ask something like, "I'm thinking of starting my own company. What kind of business should it be?"

Wrong question! If you are going to start a business, it should be about what you know, what you enjoy, and, increasingly important these days, *whom* you know. I get the impression that most of these people are really asking me what new market opportunities are being created by evolving conditions. There's no question that market opportunity is important; however, it isn't, in and of itself, enough. To achieve real growth and real success, there are some other fundamental building blocks these people need to consider. "What kind of business should I start?" is indeed the wrong question. "How can I best build a successful company that makes the most of my current skills, passions, and contacts?" is a much better way for them to look at their opportunities.

My assumption is that most people reading this book already own some type of business operation or already have a pretty good idea of one they want to start. Either way, it is essential that you strive for a clear and distinctive sense of purpose.

For any small business interested in growth, a sense of purpose is the starting point from which all growth initiatives emanate. To help determine your purpose, answer these questions:

- Who is your company supposed to serve?
- What do you stand for?
- Why are you doing what you are doing?
- Why *should* you be doing what you are doing?
- What unique strengths does your organization foster?
- What is your company trying to accomplish?

If your business does not have a sense of purpose, any growth you attain is going to be the result of sporadic good fortune, a booming economy, or, most random of all, dumb luck. I've seen many growth companies experience a period of serendipity and begin to believe their own press clippings. But at the first sign of any trouble, be it from external forces or internal missteps, growth comes to a sudden and gut-wrenching halt. In my experience, this is the norm, not the exception.

Most small businesses that survive any length of time have a period of seemingly sustainable growth. However, only those organizations that are guided by the beacon of purpose successfully navigate the treacherous and ever-changing waters of today's volatile marketplace.

I sometimes call this first rule your "reason for being," but some people think that sounds too touchy-feely. So, for all you rugged lumberjack types reading this, we call it a "sense of purpose." I also talk about core values or integrity, but those words are far too loaded: They mean very different things to different people depending on the context. These different phrases, however, all get back to the idea that you and your employees have to know the answers to the questions posed earlier.

IT'S NOT ABOUT THE MONEY

What these expressions such as "sense of purpose" and "reason for being" mean is that it's about more than just making money—a lot more. If you are educated enough to be reading this book (and wise enough to see it would be helpful), you can find a job. You can make a living and put food on the table. The same goes for your employees. If it's just about money, they can work for you or they can work for somebody else down the street—what difference does it make, right?

I could quote you study after study showing all the things employees value over money, but the bottom line is that a business has to be more than just a place to make a living. A company is more than the dollars and cents that go in and come out. It has to be or it won't last, much less grow.

If it were just about the money, I could think of at least four ways I could go start a company and probably get richer than I am now. I could buy a mortuary. I could start up a few quick-lube franchises. I could open a big restaurant serving predictable food for the masses. I could get mortgages on a dozen rental properties and become a professional landlord. The problem is that none of these kinds of businesses could motivate me to get out of bed in the morning. I'd be miserable. They don't fit in with my personality, my goals, or how I want to live my life.

There are people who are well suited for these kinds of companies and who would thrive at running them. They would find ways to innovate, hire and train great people, and succeed because they find meaning in what they do. They have a sense of purpose. For me, the only sense of purpose I would have would be to make more money.

By the same token, the vast majority of people couldn't do what I do for a living and feel good about it. If the relentless travel didn't get to them, getting on stage in front of 1,500 people probably would.

Money is a way to keep score. Money is a way to finance expansion. Money is a way to measure growth, provide incentives, and reward success. However, it cannot be the prime reason your company exists. If it is, you had better find a new direction and a new reason for being. Yes, of course, we all want to make money. That's a given. The more ambitious among us would also like to become comfortably wealthy or even stinkin' rich. That's okay, as long as it is a by-product of a great business that inspires you and others to excel. If wealth is the only goal, you will be a rudderless ship.

IT'S NOT JUST WHAT YOU KNOW

A bit of caution is in order, however, when I say you should do what you know. Some people will tell you to follow what you love, and in some cases that can be good advice. But not always. Just because you love to drink doesn't mean you should own a bar. In fact, you'll probably be a better bar owner if you don't drink at all. Just because you like to go to parties doesn't mean you should be a caterer. Just because you watch ESPN all day doesn't mean you should aspire to owning a professional sports franchise. You may be good at designing print advertisements, so perhaps this means you would be good at running a creative boutique. It doesn't mean, however, that you would find the same sense of purpose in running a full-scale advertising agency, since your true drive applies to only one small part of the business.

Would-be business owners often mistake their love for a product or service as a sign of opportunity. However, most of the truly successful growth leaders I know eventually find a greater passion in other facets of their business. You may start with a product or service bent, but it normally takes a new-found passion to reach the next level—a passion for helping people realize their dreams, a passion for a fanatical base of devoted customers, or a passion for building something good, tangible, and lasting.

The greatest sustained success I ever led was as president of a uniform apparel company. Our primary product was aprons. Instead of the cheap, white, nearly disposable "back-of-house" aprons you would regularly see on kitchen staff, these were the more substantial, expensive "front-of-house" aprons worn by wait staffs, convenience store clerks, and the Wal-Marts/Home Depots of the world. While I never articulated this sentiment at the time, it is now clear to me that I never loved aprons. I loved the challenge of filling a void. I loved building a culture that others admired and of which I was proud. I loved helping other people make money so that I in turn could make money. I was passionate about our sense of purpose, but it really had very little to do with the product we produced.

Purpose Begets the "Big Idea"

In 1999, sisters Sarah Speare and Lesley Lutyens decided they wanted to start a business together. Both 40-something women had careers at the time. Lesley designed a line of children's knitwear, and Sarah was a former graphic designer who was running a nonprofit organization. "We had both had some success in the past and we knew how to do things right," said Sarah.

Yet, they really yearned to do something big. They weren't sure what that big idea would be, but nonetheless, they started on a methodical journey, investigating where their skills and interests might intersect with a sizable opportunity. "We really did our homework from the very start," said Sarah.

Eventually, the sisters did decide on a few key parameters for their start-up:

- It had to be at least a $100 million idea.
- It had to be built around a team of the very best minds they could attract.
- It had to be a concept that was simple to understand and easy to convey.
- It had to be relatively free of well-entrenched competitors.
- It had to be both interesting and challenging to them.

They decided on the pet industry because they both loved dogs and the industry appeared to be wide open to creative ideas. They started by developing concepts for dog toys, which interested them both, but decided the odds of ratcheting up to over $100 million seemed daunting. Lesley knew kids' clothes and, therefore, understood that success often hinged on the fickle fancies of fashion.

Then one day it hit them. One sister was enjoying a breath mint while the other was indulging in a chocolate bar. That's it . . . pet

(Continued)

candy! The idea was solid, and further investigation only fueled their creative fires. Over 60 million Americans own pets, and they spend nearly $34 billion on them. Yet, no one had developed a brand of pet treats, pet candies, or breath mints available where you buy human treats and candies—at the checkout line. It was a whole new category. It seemed hard to believe the market was so wide open, but there it was. Doggy breath mints next to the human gum and mints, an idea whose time had come. "The more we looked around, the more we realized this was the big opportunity we'd been looking for."

By the end of 1999, Chomp Inc. was incorporated and product development began in earnest. By 2001, Sniffers and Yip Yaps were ready for in-store placement. Initial sales into traditional pet distribution worked well. However, placing a new impulse item where impulse items for humans already existed proved to be the best idea of all. Bed Bath & Beyond bought into the concept early. Major grocery retailers soon followed. Chomp scrambled to meet the growing demand, and sales took off. Revenue is approaching $10 million a year. Their products are available in more than 20,000 retail stores. They have managed to attract a number of big hitters from the "people food" industry to their executive team and board. Over $3 million in outside capital has been raised. Given the market potential and the strong internal structure, their initial $100 million goal seems very doable.

"Once we had some success, we were constantly tempted to deviate from our initial purpose. But ultimately, we've been true to our core," said Sarah. Chomp Inc. has grown their business in a very logical fashion. They did their upfront investigations and clearly defined their core purposes in starting a business. From this process, "the big idea" emerged—not the other way around.

Many small business owners are artisans who are honing their craft. They are truly passionate about what they do. I know owners of a tree surgery company, a pool installation business, and an interior design firm who personify that passion. Once you get them started on "their thing," you can count on learning as much as you would ever need to know about sap, pH balances, and the latest spring color palette. There are plenty of music label owners who would happily spend 12 hours a day talking about nothing but music. That obsession can be a detriment in itself if these people have no idea what's going on outside their little niche, but if they don't have blinders on, the sense of purpose that they have can be a powerful driver of their business.

There are probably more than a few people reading this book who run a company they wouldn't have started had it been their choice. Maybe you are now the head of a business that has been in the family for ages. Maybe you were a white knight who took over a firm because you knew you thought you could turn it around. Maybe your equity stake made you the boss when nobody else wanted to run the business.

If you have been thrown into a company that you can't get excited about, you have two choices: You can either back off and hire a leader with more passion for the business, or you can latch on to something that will make that company's path exciting to you. Develop a new product line, find a new market, or find others with whom to partner. One way or another, you have to develop a reason for being and believe in it, or you will never be able to grow a great staff, your customer base, and your profits. Frankly, at some point, you probably won't even be able to get out of bed.

You can't fake a sense of purpose. Maybe you can get away with a little fudging in other aspects of your business, but not this one. You can't just wake up one day and say, "Okay, today we are going to establish some strong core values!" This is not something you hire a consultant to write for you. Yes, a consultant may be able to help you see your sense of purpose as it now exists, but he or she can't give you a packaged set of core values. That would be like trying to plant flowers in a hole dug in concrete. After a few days, the flowers would wither and die because they are not rooted in anything. Your sense of purpose needs to spring from within.

DEVELOP A CLEAR AND DIFFERENTIATING CULTURE

What do I mean by *culture?* I'm not sure I can define it, but I know it when I see it. For me, culture refers to an underlying set of values, beliefs, standards, priorities, and attitudes. When tallied, the sum of these parts becomes your unique culture. It permeates everything that you do and everyone you influence. In the end, your culture answers the question, "What really matters around here?"

The smaller the organization, the more the culture is reflective of the owner(s). Later in this chapter, we look at two companies who went from tiny start-ups to giant success stories and see how that affected their ability to keep their culture intact. In the early days, though, you can bet that the company's personality will be much like that of its owner. If you project a personality that turns off customers, you can bet that your company culture will, too.

I have a client who is one of the nicest people you could ever meet when she is outside of her well-established, but stagnant, professional services firm. This niceness is almost to a fault in her personal relations: She apologizes for things that aren't even remotely her fault. When I visit, she is overly concerned about my personal comfort. But in her business, she is the exact opposite. Maybe it's because of insecurity, feelings of being overwhelmed, or just boredom, but whatever causes there are come together at the office. It would be kind to say she is less than cordial to her employees. She never yells, but she never smiles either. She rarely says something as simple as "please" or "thank you" to the people working for her. Commands are barked into an intercom system repeatedly throughout the day. She avoids face-to-face contact at all costs. Here's this really nice woman who, for whatever reason, turns grumpy and gruff when she gets to work. She is obviously capable of being pleasant, but she isn't. As a result, she has a company that reflects how she behaves.

Her excuse is that she is just being expedient and efficient, but it comes across as being short and demanding. So that culture then becomes engrained, and the employees do the same things to their vendors, customers, and even potential new hires. Customers misinterpret their stoicism as indifference. Partners misinterpret their concentration on the task at hand for lack of empathy. Potential all-stars are often put off by the tone of the interview process. A friendly woman with an unfriendly company is a real shame. Despite my repeated advice, this undesirable culture is so ingrained, I see little chance of them ever achieving sustained growth.

Contrast this with a company I often buy from called CD Baby. I've never met founder Derek Sivers, but I feel like I know him. He was a musician and a circus performer. He helped people get their independent music out; then the Internet came along, and now he has a $10 million company. The culture there is one of mission-driven fun. People buy recorded music to enhance their life and give them pleasure, so that culture is reflected in what the company does at every turn. Here's one small example—the confirming e-mail a first-time buyer receives.

Steven—

Thanks for your order with CD Baby!

Your CDs have been gently taken from our CD Baby shelves with sterilized contamination-free gloves and placed onto a satin pillow. A team of 50 employees inspected your CDs and polished them to make sure they were in the best possible condition before mailing. Our packing specialist from Japan lit a candle and a hush fell over the crowd as he put your CDs into the finest gold-lined box that money can buy.

We all had a wonderful celebration afterwards and the whole party marched down the street to the post office where the entire town of Portland waved "Bon Voyage!" to your package, on its way to you, in our private CD Baby jet on this day, Tuesday, April 27th.

I hope you had a wonderful time shopping at CD Baby. We sure did. Your picture is on our wall as "Customer of the Year." We're all exhausted but can't wait for you to come back to CDBABY.COM!!

Thank you once again,

Derek Sivers, president, CD Baby

This culture is in keeping with their company mind-set, the type of customers they want, and the kind of staff they are trying to attract. This culture is a perfect fit for their fun business.

Fun by itself, however, won't make up for inefficiency, lack of capability, poor targeting, or a bad business plan. Fun also has to be appropriate to the business segment. I'm not ready for a wacky attorney or a by-the-seat-of-the-pants CPA. Several times I've visited a certain privately owned ice cream shop in New England where the owner has a true passion for making unique and delicious flavors of ice cream: He is a true artisan. Yet, this guy is a Gloomy Gus. He is never rude, but I never get a sense of joy either. His small talk seems forced, and he rarely greets anyone with a smile. I just love the ice cream, so this is not as big a deal to me as a customer as it would be to a mom or dad with a minivan full of kids. But I know this guy is missing a more complete sense of purpose. His eye is on the wrong target. His purpose should be family joy, not well-produced, high-fat sweets.

If you see that your personality is a bad match for the business unit you lead, then you need to develop your persona and make sure the image you project is a reflection of your sense of purpose. I'm not suggesting that you change your personality; however, I am suggesting that you accentuate the positive and appropriate personality traits you undoubtedly possess. Many successful growth entrepreneurs, for example, lean to the introversion side. However, these successful organizational developers understand the vital importance of summoning their latent outgoingness. For some, it is a struggle, but it is worth it. My Gloomy Gus ice cream maker may be a sourpuss outside the shop, but I think he could find a way to turn on the charm for his customers if he put the effort into it. Do you want to know what the culture you are fostering looks and feels like right now? Ask your employees (or former employees) and customers what they think. You might be surprised at what you hear.

WHAT'S YOUR CULTURE?

Different cultures are appropriate for different businesses, and it is important that the two are a good match. Because the owner's demeanor often determines the culture, especially in the early days, it is imperative that you are aware of the influence you wield in this key area.

See if you recognize any of these culture archetypes in you or your business:

- *The Star Trek culture:* You are boldly going where no one has gone before. You are flying at the speed of light, driven, on a mission, and deadly serious.
- *The Willy Wonka and the Chocolate Factory culture:* You are all about creativity and innovation and building a place of wonder. Big smiles abound.
- *The Dead Poets' Society culture:* You are nurturing and developmental. You are aiming for organic growth, with a focus on people and service to the greater good.
- *The Amadeus culture:* You are thought of as a stark-raving-mad genius who is larger than life. You fill your team with raw talent and give them and yourself wide latitude. The end result is more important than the means of getting there.
- *The Patton culture:* Business is blood and guts. You manage through intimidation but earn respect by leading the charge and inspiring success by example.
- *The Millionaire Next Door culture:* (I depart from the movie theme on this one.) You are staid and steady, with your eye on the prize. You are counting the beans and taking only the risks you are sure will pay off. Hands-on hard work and determination are key.

A Willy Wonka culture is great for an ad agency but terribly inappropriate for an accounting firm. The Patton culture may work great for a private security company, but it would be a disaster in a child care center. There is no right or wrong culture for your business. But it has to be authentic, and it has to be appropriate.

I admit I have some bias against the command and control culture, but I do have to admit it can get results at times. I once had two key clients to whom I sold the same basic products. Both had sales of approximately $5 to $10 million when we established a relationship. It was obvious to me that both of these customers were capable of tremendous growth. Within eight years, the organization with the more nurturing, touchy-feely culture surpassed $40 million in revenue. The Pattonesque competitor was the direct antithesis. They seemed to break every tenet of what a modern growth company's culture should be. I regularly saw employees in tears and watched a phone ripped out of the wall during one of the owner's frequent tirades. This organization reached a very profitable $25 million in revenue in the same period. You would be hard pressed to tell "Mr. Patton" that he didn't do it right. What's my point? There are many cultures that can lead to growth, but all things being equal, it's a heck of a lot more pleasant for everyone concerned if you adopt a culture that sees people as people, not as human capital.

THE IMPORTANCE OF MYTHOLOGY

Any company that has been around for a while has plenty of stories to tell. In the early years especially, private businesses go through all kinds of challenges and experience all kinds of mishaps and thrills. These stories become part of the company mythology and are key to defining who they are.

Every culture in the world has its mythology, lore, and legends that speak to who they are. Many times, these stories teach us values, reinforce our ideals, or highlight struggles we must all overcome. Other times, they give us a historical grounding in where we came from. These stories exist for a reason: They highlight a culture's aspirations and what it views as worthy and righteous. The Mayan and Aztec legends are still told today in large swaths of Latin America, while the legends of King Arthur, Arabian Nights, and the Greek gods still have a profound impact around the world.

Here in America, we have our own home-grown mythology. It permeates our law, our politics, our business, how our religions are practiced, and most other aspects of our lives.

For instance, Paul Bunyan is a uniquely American hero. He took on the frontier with his bare hands and represents the rugged American individualist who won't give up. Many of our other legendary figures display similar traits: Davy Crockett, Daniel Boone, and Johnny Appleseed all shaped America in a way that is far larger than their actual accomplishments. Davy Crockett served in Congress, but that's not why we know him. Instead, he was a great storyteller who enthralled audiences with tales of fighting off bears, protecting the innocent, and otherwise taming the frontier. Dying at the Alamo secured his position as an American legend forever.

We hand down stories of these brave, odds-defying Americans whether they were on the right side of the law (Annie Oakley), the wrong side (Butch Cassidy and the Sundance Kid), or somewhere in between (Wyatt Earp). This particular type of character is a polar opposite of the heroes in most Asian cultures. Their legends build teams, they save the honor of their ancestors, and they win only by rallying the troops to a consensus. It's all about *The Seven Samurais,* not *The Last Samurai.* American mythology reflects rugged individualism, self-confidence, overcoming great odds, and going it alone. Perhaps this explains why much of the world has a hard time replicating our entrepreneurial spirit.

Our other point of cultural mythology comes from the founding of our country. Search for "founding fathers" in Google, and you'll get more than 450,000 results. Our founding fathers' words are used on a daily basis to rationalize actions on the right and left and everywhere in between. People such as Ben Franklin, Thomas Jefferson, George Washington, and Alexander Hamilton still have a profound influence on where our country is and where it is going. You can follow that path to the next legendary leader of 100 years later, Abe Lincoln, who again embodied all that we hold dear. The ideas these people stood for, especially honesty, equality, and a down-to-earth realness, are still qualities we hold in the highest regard in choosing a leader today.

FINDING YOUR OWN MYTHOLOGY

So what's your story? What makes your company's founding and growth special? What stories define who you are and how you got here?

To help illustrate this point to groups I speak to, I often use my own family as an analogy. I have a 13-year-old son. This teenager can give you a pretty good synopsis of how my wife and I met, what happened on the first date, what happened in the first year, and the trials and tribulations leading up to the point of his eventual birth. He's got that story down to a short and sweet, humorous three- to four-minute tale. Like his dad, he likes to tell stories, and he's pretty good at it.

What fascinates me about the story, however, is that it bears little resemblance to what happened. And that's okay. For him, it is a unifying element. For him, it is a story with a message. He wasn't even born yet, and still he feels as if he were part of the team.

All growth companies have a foundation story. I'm not altogether sure I know why, but they do—all of them. It doesn't matter if you leave out the part about the original partner absconding with the seed capital or that you started off in insurance and ended up in ball bearings. Those need not be part of the lore, legend, and mythology surrounding your business. If you don't have a good foundation story, I'm going to suggest you form one. Maybe it gives us the same kind of grounding our national mythology gives us. It's hard to say exactly. But I am sure that every successful growth company has a well-crafted mythology surrounding its foundation and growth.

I'm sure there are a few skeptics who look at all of this as new age mumbo-jumbo and think it's really just about the products and the service. A good story can't define a company or a brand. However, how many of these have you heard to the point where they are permanently stuck in your head?

- Ray Kroc, at 52 years old, invested his life savings to become a milkshake machine distributor. One day he visited a hamburger joint called McDonald's that was using eight of the machines at once. He liked the way they had standardized processes and said, "You could do this anywhere!" He joined them as a partner and opened the second McDonald's in 1955. A worldwide icon was born, and the rest is history.
- Bill Gates dropped out of college and started Microsoft in his garage with Paul Allen. Neither of them had any business or management experience. The company moved to Seattle when it had 12 employees and hired Steve Ballmer, another college dropout. Before long, the company had created over 250 millionaires, and Gates became the richest man on earth.
- In 1971, Rollin King and Herb Kelleher got together in a bar and sketched out an idea for a different kind of airline. Kelleher backed the project with $10,000 of his own money. The goals were to leave on time, arrive on time, offer a lower price than anyone else, and make sure everyone had a good time in the process. With competitors

trying to keep them from launching, the company literally took years to get off the ground. When a cash crunch forced the choice of selling one of his four planes or laying off 70 employees, Kelleher sold the plane. To settle a disagreement over an ad slogan, Kelleher arm-wrestled the rival airline's CEO. He was known to show up for company speeches dressed as Elvis or the Easter Bunny. The company has been profitable every year since 1973, and when all the other airlines buckled in the wake of the September 11, 2001, attacks, Southwest didn't lay off a single employee.

I know these are all big company examples, but they all started out as fast-growth small companies. I bring them up because they show the power of building a good mythology. You can be the Ray Kroc in your niche or segment, propagating your own legends that will be passed down from employee to employee and customer to customer.

Figure out your mythology. Leave in the good parts, take out the bad parts, and create compelling tales that make a point. Tell people about the defining moments, the overcoming of adversity, and the beating of the long odds. Tell us what made you as a company who you are. Before you know it, you'll have your own great American success story.

These legends are something to latch on to, something that transcends the slogans, the mission statements, and other hit-or-miss verbiage. They provide direction and a sense of belonging to your employees and partners. They give reporters a narrative to talk about. They guide your marketing and your planning. They remind you of both your grounding and your future.

Once you have these legends pared to compelling tales you can rattle off consistently, keep talking about them. Make sure every new employee hears them. Make them a part of your training. Make them a part of every interview. If everyone connected to the company knows these tales by heart, you will have a powerful message. You will also have a serious leg up on your competitors. Also, keep your ears open for the anti-myth. I knew a company where the mythology that was passed from the old guard to the new guard entailed dramatic instances of "sticking it to the client." Regular water cooler conversations included tales of buried expenses and inflated time sheets. The mythology perpetuated an "us versus them" attitude toward customers. Needless to say, this company is no longer with us.

I have a friend who has traveled the world reviewing hundreds of hotels in different countries. Surprisingly, the company he thinks has the best identity is not the Four Seasons or Ritz-Carlton, but The Oberoi Group, based in India. They are known for the stunning luxury and professional service that are assumed at this level of hospitality in their properties scattered from Mumbai to Melbourne. What he finds most fascinating, however, is that if you ask any employee of that company to tell you what the founder, M. S. Oberoi, was like, they will immediately tell you a favorite story that defines his character. Interestingly, his biography is much like an American success story: He started off poor, worked his way up from a busboy position, bought a single hotel with the help of some of his wife's pawned jewelry, almost went bankrupt several times, but then eventually became hugely successful. In the middle are many tales of overcoming great odds and developing innovations that kept him ahead of competitors, including deep-pocketed international chains.

The maids and gardeners are required to learn these stories, not because they are some kind of hero worship, but because they define where the company came from and why it matters.

There is another layer on top of this, however, in that every single hotel has a story as well, which the customer-facing employees are known to rattle off every chance they get. If the property is in a building that is 250 years old, the employees know all the major events and turning points that occurred in the past within those walls (edited for interest). If the resort was built five years ago, they will tell you how the architecture was inspired, what the statues out front represent, and where the artifacts in the lobby came from. Everything has a story, and everyone who works there knows it. It's a core part of the training, and nobody talks to a guest until he or she has it all down.

I'm a big fan of the Ritz-Carlton chain of luxury hotels. In fact, I give a great example of where they shine in Chapter 6. But I don't know the Ritz-Carlton foundation story. Maybe they are so big that they don't need to push it now. It's hard to argue with their success. I still come at this from a small business person's perspective. To me, the foundation story is merely an example of a thousand other ways in which a sense of purpose becomes instilled in an organization.

WHAT DO YOU STAND FOR?

When you talk about what you stand for, you need to get specific. Don't bore your employees and everyone else with corporate babble and doublespeak. People don't get fired up about "creating value for our stakeholders," "leveraging our core competencies," or other generic phrases that belong in boring annual reports. Leave that for the corporate suits who are trying not to offend anyone.

Give your employees, customers, and partners a reason to care. Tell them why you are different. Tell them why what you do matters.

TWO PARALLEL PATHS

Let's look at two legendary companies that came from far different backgrounds but have a lot in common: Hewlett-Packard (H-P) and Ben & Jerry's. Both were once scrappy little companies founded by two people with strong beliefs. The legends were a big part of the brand—the founders were larger than life. In the end, after nasty struggles about who they were and where their future was going, the identities of both got swallowed up by larger entities.

Hewlett-Packard—Innovation in All Areas

In 1938, Stanford graduates Bill Hewlett and Dave Packard formed their own electronics company just four years out of college. With $538 in working capital, they started out in a garage behind a house in Palo Alto, California. They flipped a coin to see whose name would come first in the formal partnership name. As the company grew, the founders became known for "management by walking around" and "management by objective," both unusual practices at the time.

When the partners began building their headquarters, they constructed the building so that it might be converted into a grocery store if the business failed to grow. The product line continued to expand, and revenue topped $2 million, then $5 million, then $28 million as the company went public in 1957, with around 1,800 employees on board. All employees with six months of service or more received a stock grant. The company then moved to a 50-acre hilltop site complete with horseshoe pits, volleyball courts, and a company cafeteria.

In the late 1960s, H-P advertised the first personal computer and introduced the concept of flexible schedules to its offices. The company passed $2 billion in revenue in the

1970s, $11 billion in the 1980s, and $47 billion in the 1990s. In 2000, the company hit number 13 on the Fortune 500. Despite its meteoric rise, everyone understood what H-P stood for. Everyone still derived a sense of purpose from those two innovative tinkerers in a garage.

In 2001, cofounder Bill Hewlett died. Later that same year, with growth hitting a wall, the managers of H-P and Compaq announced an intended merger. A nasty proxy battle ensued between H-P management, led by CEO Carly Fiorina and a group of investors headed by the founders' families. In the end, after a prolonged PR and advertising battle, management squeaked by with a win. We can speculate that the merger caused a slowdown or the slowdown caused the merger, but it's no secret that H-P's big growth days are behind it. Much of the R&D budget is going into projects that will have an immediate payoff, not ones that will open whole new markets five years from now. With the founders and their families no longer having any influence, a company founded on the principles of innovation and invention is now finding that its sense of purpose has changed. While the jury is still out, I'm willing to bet this change of purpose will not be for the better.

Ben & Jerry's—Two Hippies Prove That Good Guys Can Finish First

In 1977, two ex-hippie high school buddies named Ben Cohen and Jerry Greenfield put together $12,000 to start an ice cream parlor. Their initial choice was bagels, but the machinery was too expensive. Part of their training was a $5 Penn State correspondence course in ice cream making: They received straight A's because the test was open book. They chose Burlington, Vermont, as the second-best place to start their ice cream venture, after finding that their first choice—Saratoga Springs, New York—already had an ice cream parlor.

They moved into a renovated gas station in 1978 and marked their one-year anniversary with a "free scoop day," a tradition that continues nationwide today. The company grew at a rate exceeding 100 percent per year, and in 1985, the founders established the Ben & Jerry's Foundation to contribute to community-oriented projects, to be funded with 7.5 percent of the company's annual pretax profits. Ben & Jerry's wild flavors caught on with the public. Cherry Garcia, named after the Grateful Dead member, became a big hit. After the stock market crash in 1987, Ben & Jerry's vans pulled up to Wall Street to serve free scoops of "That's Life" and "Economic Crunch."

Ben & Jerry's began to be held up as a standard for good corporate behavior. Besides the institutionalized profit portion that went to charity, the company codified the salary spread between CEO and the lowest paid worker and regularly supported a variety of social causes. The company introduced Rainforest Crunch ice cream to encourage sustainable growth and preservation in the rainforest regions. One of their brownie factories employed only disadvantaged workers, and when Vermont dairy farmers got pummeled by volatile prices, the company donated a half-million dollars to the family farmers who supplied the milk for Ben & Jerry's ice cream. In 1988, President Reagan named Ben and Jerry Small Business Persons of the Year in a White House ceremony. Jerry put on the only suit he owned for the occasion.

In 1993, sales hit $140 million, and the company ran an essay contest to find an outside CEO. First place would get the job. Second place received a lifetime supply of ice cream.

In the late 1990s, sales topped $200 million, and a Harris Interactive poll showed Ben & Jerry's as the number five most reputable company in the United States, with a number one ranking in the "social responsibility" category.

After Ben & Jerry's sales hit $237 million in 1999, Unilever made an offer to buy the company. Although Ben Cohen opposed the sale, Jerry and the company's board agreed, and the deal was done. Many fans of the company were appalled, but final terms created a separate board of directors, a commitment to continue all social programs, and a promise to continue eco-friendly packaging initiatives. As many expected, however, some of the social programs have quietly disappeared in the years since, including the 7.5 percent of profits going to charity. With the founders no longer holding the reins and the company now just a division of one of the world's biggest conglomerates, time will tell how much of the original sense of purpose will survive. Here again, a company propelled by purpose appears to have lost its direction.

Ben & Jerry's and H-P are two companies you would think are as different as night and day. However, both share a host of commonalities: a strong mythology, dynamic founders, well-established reputations, and a devoted customer base. Yet, all of these commonalities can be traced back to the single most important trait they shared: a strong sense of purpose established at the very beginning, in a garage filled with little more than dreams and desire.

For any business interested in reaching another level, purpose is the place to start. In fact, I would submit this could be said about any human endeavor. Think back on any remarkable organizational achievement, whether it is in history or in your own personal life, and a sense of purpose is always the first step. John Kennedy said, "We're going to put a man on the moon before the end of the decade," and suddenly NASA had its purpose. My mother and her friends decided they were going to save a historic church in Fernandina Beach, Florida, and within two years, garnered a state grant of over half a million dollars. As you look at the business you have today or the one you plan to start tomorrow, remember that establishing and honing your sense of purpose is the first key rung in your ladder to growth.

SUGGESTED NEXT STEPS

1. Ask successful business owners you admire in your industry, community, family, and so on what their initial purpose was in starting their company. Find out if their initial purpose is still in place today.

2. List on a sheet of paper your 10 most unique personal strengths. Ask yourself if these strengths are apparent in your organization. If not, why?

3. Write down your organization's sense of purpose, including whom you want to serve, how you serve them, and the highest goal of the organization. Be sure it is clear, unique, and credible.

4. Share your thoughts on sense of purpose with others close to the business. Ask them if it is clear, unique, and credible.

5. Using a voice recorder, listen to yourself telling your company's foundation story. Be sure that it is interesting, indicative, and conveys an overall lesson to be learned.

4

RULE 2:
THOROUGHLY
UNDERSTAND THE
MARKETPLACE

You know the world is going crazy when the best rapper is a White guy, the best golfer is a Black guy, the tallest guy in the NBA is Chinese, the Swiss hold the America's Cup, and France is accusing the U.S. of arrogance . . .

—Chris Rock

The word *predictable* isn't of much use any more, especially when it comes to business. Competitors, partners, and customers shape-shift and flow constantly. The days when you could see where every competitive threat was coming from and what it was likely to be are over. The 10-year strategic plan has become useless, and even the five-year strategic plan is mostly a business version of science fiction writing.

To grow a business, you need superior market intelligence. You need a macroview of the changing marketplace.

This is difficult enough when things are standing still. But with the landscape changing every month or every week, it takes real diligence.

The big companies, as good as they are at measuring external threats, still get surprised at every turn. Apple, once just a computer maker, is quickening the demise of music retailers through its music portal iTunes. Samsung and LG, in the space of about two years, took a machete to Nokia's wireless phone market share. It took only one low-carb diet craze to wipe billions off the market value of a wide variety of pasta, rice, and baked goods producers. Meanwhile, privately held Atkins Nutritionals sold an estimated $200 million of food products in 2003. Ford ignored hybrid electric car engines for years, but now they are compelled to license the technology from Toyota for a whole line of new vehicles.

If these things are happening to the big guys, what chance do you have?

First, it doesn't happen to *all* the big companies. General Electric, the world's biggest conglomerate, often seems to be as nimble as many small entrepreneurial organizations. Microsoft may not be growing as fast as before, but the company still manages to win new markets and be a cash-generating monster. Dell has kept up an impressively long streak of beating the competition. There are plenty of other organizations that always seem to be one step ahead of the pack. They expand into a new market just as it is starting to take off. It may look like magic or good luck, but it's not. These companies have superior market intelligence.

LITTLE GUYS CAN PLAY THAT GAME, TOO

You don't have to be a giant corporation with millions invested in market research to get it right, however. What you need is that seemingly uncanny ability to recognize what customers are looking for and how to respond to it. Among the 2003 Inc. 500 winners, 84 percent had started their companies without the benefit of any formal market research. What they did do was figure out a way to grow rapidly by understanding the marketplace.

Superior market intelligence is not some mystical psychic power. Instead, it is an organization's ability to first recognize, then adapt to, significant changes in the marketplace.

Some say that what makes an expert an expert is not more knowledge or even an ability to explain that knowledge. It is the ability to see patterns where others cannot. In other words, an expert has the ability to distinguish between a coincidence and a trend, between a fad and a phenomenon, and between a real opportunity and a potential waste of resources.

BALANCE THE INTERNAL AND EXTERNAL

Small enterprises have a big advantage over big ones when it comes to internal focus. You don't build up big organizational silos that inhibit cooperation and idea flow. You usually have a better handle on your cash position, your monthly expenses, and marketing costs. If you're developing your people correctly, you have a good sense of all your employees' strengths and weaknesses. You know your products or services like you know your own family. As a leader of the organization, you generally have a better handle on the day-to-day operation of your company than a corporate CEO ever will.

All of this can be a positive, but it can also get in the way of your external focus. You need to regularly step back and look at the big picture. Ask yourself:

- How is your company really faring in the marketplace?
- How do you stack up against current and potential competitors?

- What innovations are the other guys making that you haven't put into place?
- What could you be doing that would give you an edge over them?
- What other markets, product lines, or services could you develop to grow your business?
- What is happening in the macroworld, beyond your own vertical industry?
- What are your customers saying about you? Your competitors?
- What actions can you observe, among your current and future customers, that speak louder than their words?

ARE YOU THE ARTISAN OR
THE ENTREPRENEUR?

Regardless of the kind of company you are running, you need to ask yourself this question: Am I a toolmaker or a manager of toolmakers? In other words, consider whether you are an artisan or an entrepreneur. The answer is important because it is extremely difficult, if not downright impossible, to grow your business if you are both.

If you are a one-person operation, you have no choice but to wear both hats. If you want to grow a company, however, you need to decide what your role is going to be. Then you need to hire someone to take the other role. If you are the chief engineer, lead inventor, or head architect at your firm, somebody else needs to be reading the signals and looking for opportunities. You are focused on the immediate tasks at hand.

If, however, you are the one pushing for growth, you can't allow yourself to become mired in the day-to-day. Most of your time should be spent on finding new customers, increasing your opportunities with current customers, building new markets, and developing products or services that can increase your revenue.

A MACROVIEW

Listening to your customers is one step, but it won't give you the big picture. For that you need a macroview. You need to know what is happening in your industry, what is happening to the industries connected to your industry, and which potential companies have the ability to get a piece of your industry. You also need time to step back and consider whether your industry is still doing things in a way that makes sense.

On the whole, small businesses are lousy at seeing the macroview. We become so myopically focused on our internal operations that we don't take the time to regularly consider the important fundamental shifts taking place in the general marketplace.

Some markets are just dying. They're not going to come back, at least in their current form. If you are in one of them now, there are only two paths to follow. You can either stick it out and be the last one standing, or you can find a way to use your assets, skills, and people for new opportunities. Those who don't see their own extinction coming are going to be blindsided and could lose everything.

Tower Records should not have been surprised when the company started to slide toward bankruptcy. After all, the company's whole appeal was that its stores had a wider selection of music than anyone else. But if I can buy every CD there is from my computer chair, sampling any of them before buying, what does that do to Tower's reason for being? I'm not trying to pick on Tower Records because any of us can be made irrelevant at any time by someone who has found a good way to do what we're doing cheaper, faster, better, or all three.

A Uniform Business?

In the 1980s, I became president of that small apron manufacturer. The aprons we produced were not the type people buy at retail stores to wear in their kitchens, but the kind you see employees wearing in bars, restaurants, hotels, grocery stores, and the like. These garments have a dual purpose: protecting an employee's clothes and serving as an identity tool for the business. Aprons serve as a highly effective uniform look at a relatively low cost.

In a manufacturing-based economy, the word *uniform* connoted something different than it does today—a shirt, a pair of pants, or maybe even a hat that was worn in a grimy industrial environment. Invariably, these uniforms were provided by an industrial laundry service, which had been contracted by the employer to regularly deliver clean, well-fitted garments. The employer paid for this service for a primarily male workforce. This system worked because the employees were of one sex, stayed in their jobs for a relatively long period of time, and were centralized in a single location, making distribution of the garments efficient.

As we moved into a more service-based economy, all of this began to change. Women began entering the workforce in droves, and people began to take jobs for shorter durations. Much assembly work was moved offshore and, by the mid-1980s, the majority of jobs were in the service sector, the fastest growing employment segment. The existing modelof a uniform—what it was, where it was purchased, who paid for it, who wore it, and even why they wore it—was changing forever.

(Continued)

The lowly apron became the perfect uniform solution for the emerging service-based economy, where employers were looking for a low-cost, unisex way to protect and identify their diverse, short-term, decentralized workforces. It was a fundamental shift that anyone who had a vested interest in aprons or uniforms should have seen early. Yet, very few did.

Two leading apron companies that we competed with directly were small businesses, although they were many times bigger than we were when I took over the management of the company. I knew both presidents from industry functions and the occasional, "Can you help us out on a fabric overage?" that periodically cropped up.

HINDSIGHT IS 20/20

It is now apparent that neither of the two leading apron companies had a macroview of the changes in the overall market and the opportunities they presented. One would have described her company as "making tea aprons for maids and waitresses sold through specialty retailers and department stores." The other would have described his company as "manufacturing sewn products made of woven fabrics (including aprons) that could be sold to screen printers." But neither would have said: "We provide the growing service economy with a low-cost substitute for traditional uniforms."

Thanks to our ability to see and react to the macrochanges taking place in the general market, sales at our small apron company grew more than 2,000 percent in less than seven years. Our growth represented a tremendous loss of opportunity for our

(Continued)

(Continued)

chief competitors—one failed to grow in the apron market, and the other eventually went out of business.

THE LESSON LEARNED

Why did this happen? Not because we were so smart, but instead because the other guys were so slow to first recognize, and then adapt to, fundamental changes in the marketplace. I would also argue that it was my relative ignorance about the "proper" day-to-day operation of this kind of business that gave me the time to see the macroview. Had I known more about fabric utilization software or the latest sewing machine attachments, I might never have taken the time to consider the fundamental, near-term future of our company and industry. Ultimately, seeing the macro proved to be our most important competitive advantage.

You can't prevent the market from changing. But by having a macroview, you are able to cut down the time between realization and action, between attack and counterattack, or between defense and offense.

GOOD IDEAS CAN COME FROM ANYWHERE

In Chapter 3, I discussed your need to have a real reason for being and to develop the stories and legends that define what you are and where you came from. I've heard hundreds of these stories while talking to owners and managers of growing companies. It is amazing how much of their success has come from simply seeing and grabbing an opportunity before someone else sees it.

Consider how these runaway successes were the result of fairly simple ideas:

- Swiffer dust mop
- eBay
- Priceline or Hotwire
- Origins
- Starbucks
- Mail Boxes, Etc. (now UPS Store)
- Jiffy Lube
- Mosquito Magnet
- NetJet
- Whole Foods/Wild Oats
- Blackboard
- Build-a-Bear
- Maxim or Lucky magazines
- LendingTree
- CarMax

These are all breakthrough products or companies that, when launched, represented a major shift from the norm. Not coincidentally, they also all have respectable growth stories. If you don't recognize some of them, do a Web search and see what they're about. Each of them went from an idea to millions of dollars in what seems in hindsight to be the blink of an eye. There are hundreds of others like them, most working under the radar, doing business-to-business or infrastructure work that is out of the public eye. Do some reading (more on that later), and you'll find some inspiring stories about the power of an idea.

Innovations such as Velcro, Post-It Notes, Nylon, and Netflix are the stuff of business school case studies. They also illustrate that a lot of great products and services were either the result of failures in their intended use or were the by-product of "aha" moments that now seem obvious.

Swiss inventor George de Mestral developed Velcro after investigating what made burrs stick to his dog so easily when they went for a walk. Post-it Notes were a by-product of a type of glue that just wasn't very sticky. Nylon was designed solely to make panty hose. It was quite successful in just that area, but it went on to be used in everything from pants to trampolines to bungee cords. Netflix is the one that really amazes me. They mail DVDs to customers and have eliminated the dreaded late fee. Every time a DVD from Netflix hits my mailbox, I say, "Why didn't I think of that?"

In the small business arena, thousands of companies thrive by finding novel uses for products or offering valuable services in a way that nobody has done before.

Stampp Corbin of Columbus, Ohio, found out that one organization's trash is another organization's treasure. Back in 1996, one of Corbin's largest customers for his company Resource One, told Stampp they would buy 200 new computers from him on the condition that he take their old machines off their hands. In the end, he made a hefty profit supplying the new PCs, but turned around and made three times as much refurbishing and selling the old ones. From this one transaction, the idea for RetroBox was born.

Corbin's company takes castaway computers nobody wants to deal with and erases all the data on them, eliminating any security and liability risks. By handing the machines off to someone else, companies also avoid the hassles of dealing with ever-tightening recycling laws for old electronics. RetroBox pockets a small fee for the machines, then either refurbishes or recycles them for parts. The company has grown rapidly over the years and has passed $15 million in sales. In 2003, the company was number 115 on the Inc. 500 list, with a five-year growth rate of 1,358 percent.

Stampp Corbin didn't come up with some breakthrough invention. He just found a great opportunity and capitalized on it. Fifty years ago, when you equated fast growth with small business, it was because of a brand new product. Now, many times it's not reinventing the wheel; it's putting a retread on it. Put yourself in front of Corbin's 1996 customer. Would you have found a way to solve their problem while simultaneously turning trash into treasure?

THE 50-MAG SOLUTION

Stampp Corbin was aware of the economic and environmental impact of ever-shrinking computer life spans. As a Harvard Business School graduate, Corbin was used to absorbing an abundance of information and figuring out what it meant.

This is a practice that most growth leaders get good at, however, even without such a prestigious degree. How many magazines do you go through each month? Three? Ten? Twenty? If you said anything less than 50, I'd say you run the danger of being out of touch.

If you own or run a growing enterprise, you need to be an information sponge. You need to know the business landscape intimately. You need to know your industry inside and out. You need to know your suppliers' industries, your partners' industries, and your partners' partners' industries. You need to know what's going on in the general business world—locally, regionally, nationally, and internationally. But that still doesn't cover what you should pay attention to the most: what your customers and potential customers are talking about, thinking about, and doing.

"But, Steve," you're probably saying right now, "I don't have time for that! I have a business to run!" Yes, you do, and it's probably taking up a great deal of your time. But maybe, just maybe, you have a little bit more time than you think. Perhaps you are dedicating unwarranted time to portions of your business that are about to become obsolete. Maybe you are concentrating so much on the daily grind that you're missing what is happening beyond your walls. How much time would it free up for you if the right idea enabled you to hire five more people? How much more business could you pull in if you truly understood what obstacles your customers are facing? How many more customers could you attract if you really knew who else out there is in need of your services right now?

"But, Steve," you object, "I run a company that makes industrial screws. How in the world can there be 50 magazines that are relevant to that?" Maybe they aren't all directly relevant to your company as it now stands. However, I'd be willing to bet that if you went through 50 magazines a month, within one year you would come up with plenty of ways to expand your enterprise. Maybe you would find other markets for your screws. Maybe you would discover potential customers you didn't even know were out there. Maybe you would find other products you could produce with only slight modifications to your processes. Maybe you would find partners, marketing ideas, management ideas, or even employees or acquisitions. There's no maybe about this: If you read 50 magazines a month, you are going to have a convergence of your thinking that can only serve to help you in your quest to grow. (By the way, 50 magazines a month is fewer than two a day.)

KNOW YOUR CUSTOMERS BETTER THAN THEY KNOW THEMSELVES

When I was a young boy, my brother and I sold peaches from our backyard tree door to door. By age 10, I had a pretty good handle on capitalism. The idea that "The customer is always right" was ingrained at a very young age. I had heard it from

? As my restaurant friend says, "Three customers
out the great meals they had in New Orleans dur-
Gras. What I *heard* was, 'You need to experiment
ille sausage and cayenne pepper.'" Imagine what it
for your business if just one comment sparked
t led to a successful new product or service offer-
pter 6, I describe the importance of developing
riven processes. In this instance, I'm saying your
an be the ultimate source of market intelligence.
rist author Alvin Toffler said, "The illiterate of the
not be the person who cannot read. It will be the
does not know how to learn" (New York: Ban-

GESTED NEXT STEPS

many magazines as you can afford. Then, get to
 freebies such as trade publications.

st important reasons people buy from your
ch of your principal competitors. For a reality
 employees (or others close to your business)
ar list. Compare and contrast.

mple of a time your company proved it knew
 than they know themselves. Share it through-
on.

d participate in critical associations and trade
med and share that information internally.

ondary and primary research you have. Iden-
 to plug them.

family and friends, but experience brought the message home.
To this day, in a customer service environment, I still believe
that the customer *is* always right. However, your customers
aren't always capable of articulating what you can do to
uniquely serve their wants, needs, and desires. When it comes
to growth, you've got to know customers better than they
know themselves. (See the Potato Chip Story.)

At about the same time a few years ago, two companies discovered that businesspeople were tired of carrying around so
many electronic gadgets and set about marketing a solution. A
major clothing company responded by making a pair of
dressy slacks that would carry lots of gadgets in hidden pockets. Despite favorable response to initial prototypes and an ag-
gressive advertising campaign, the product line flopped. The
pants didn't really solve the problem.

A company called Handspring (now part of Palm) decided
to make a cell phone that was also a personal data assistant
and wireless Internet device. The Treo combined items almost
everyone was carrying around into one item that could slide
into a pocket. The product was a modest hit from the start.
After Handspring merged with Palm, they made a new version
with e-mail access that was an even bigger hit.

Handspring knew their customers better than some of
those customers knew themselves. A few years ago, if the company had asked focus group members to raise their hands if
they would pay $500 or more for a 3-in-1 cell phone, few
would have said yes. In fact, I would have been one of those
people. An always on-the-go road warrior like me is the target
for such a device. But honestly, the only reason I have one is
that I was given one. For years, I have spoken on behalf of
Sprint to small business owners around the country. Sprint
gave me one of these devices, and I immediately loved it. In
fact, I can't imagine how I got along without it. Thanks in

The Potato Chip Story

When I was a younger man, I worked as an account executive and then a senior account executive at advertising agency Foote Cone & Belding's main office in Chicago. One of my accounts was Frito-Lay, so I learned more than I ever wanted to know about potato chips. One of the first things I learned was the lesson of the potato chip story.

One thing that packaged goods companies like to do is to get together a group of heavy users of a product and do a focus group. They put 10 or 12 people in a room around a table and talk about products, with marketing people watching and listening on the other side of a two-way mirror. If you asked those heavy users—heavy buyers—of potato chips what kind of chip they liked best, you always got the same answers. If you asked them if they preferred light salt, medium salt, or heavy salt, what do you think they said? Overwhelmingly, they would say, "light salt." If you asked them about heavy oil, medium oil, or light oil, most would come back with "light oil" every time.

The next step would be to do a blind taste test, sometimes literally with a blindfold, and ask them which ones they liked best. What kind of potato chips do you think they would choose? They would prefer the saltiest, oiliest ones every time.

"The customer is always right" may be good advice in the service business. But when you are talking about product development, new business initiatives, or growth plans, the customer is not always right. You need to know your customers better than they know themselves. When I was working at that same agency in Chicago, cable television was still in its infancy. The TV net works at that time were armed with studies showing that fledgling

(Continued)

cable offerings such
with the majority of
guess what? They
consumers were n
member, cable pe
homes in the mid-

Here's the mor
pate your custom
for, before they h
comes from und
about meeting th

large part to posit
Palm sold more t
model in just the f
is just a big comp
even exist as a co
with big dreams.

At one of my fa
head chef, always
their meal was an
ordered. She doe
kitchen is usuall
dozen other thin
But she knows
the food, wine,
place, and she d
rant a success.
her customers

How many
logue with? A

telling you
told me ab
ing Mardi
with andou
would do
an idea tha
ing. In Cha
customer-d
customers c

The futur
future will
person who
tam, 1984).

Su

1. Subscribe to as
   50 a month with

2. List the five m
   company and ea
   check, have your
   construct a simil

3. Find a recent exa
   customers better
   out the organizat

4. Be sure to join a
   groups. Get infor

5. Review all the sec
   tify holes and see

5

RULE 3:
BUILD AN
EFFECTIVE GROWTH
PLANNING SYSTEM

Plans are nothing; planning is everything.

—Dwight D. Eisenhower

In the world of entrepreneurial studies, few things are more actively debated among experts, scholars, and business owners alike than the role that planning plays in small business. I'm not talking about the business plan you might put together for a bank when you need money. I'm talking about the internal document the organization uses as a road map for success. Let's call it the *growth plan*.

For most experts, formal planning is an essential ingredient for any organization looking to build sustainable growth. In

2003, PriceWaterhouseCoopers interviewed over 400 CEOs of fast-growth small companies and found that nearly two-thirds have some form of growth plan in place. A 2000 Inc. Consulting survey found that 80 percent of Inc. 500 companies had a written planning process in place, while only 12 percent of all small and mid-size businesses did. Other studies have found that neither a company's industry nor its size has any significant bearing on its success or failure. Instead, it's the growth plan. In other words, it's not which game you play, but the plan to win, that matters.

Conversely, for many business owners, the "ready, fire, aim" school of business is the only way to go. This camp tends to frown at anything that attempts to paint business owners into a corner. "Plan . . . we don't need no stinkin' plan!" seems to be the strategy here.

The truth is, many small business owners don't plan very much or very well. It's a fact. It's irrefutable. The majority of small businesses don't use planning to their advantage. Are there studies that point to this fact? Yep! Am I going to recount them here? Nope!

For one thing, most of these studies rely on retrospective self-reporting. In other words, they ask successful entrepreneurs to describe how they did planning in the past. Little, if anything, is done to observe or confirm what they report to be their behavior. Some studies also look at nascent entrepreneurs, asking them to describe what motivated them to start the business and the role that planning plays in their efforts. Please check out the Potato Chip Story in Chapter 4 to see what I think about individuals' capacity for understanding their own motivations.

There is a more important gap in most attempts to understand small business planning. You see, most studies look at something academics call *strategic planning*. Therein lies the problem. That term is as loaded semantically as *card-carrying member* or *grassy knoll*. To most small business owners, strategic planning smacks of big-biz speak. As a result, the findings of any polling, surveying, or interviewing done on the subject of planning become tainted. Let me show you what I mean.

You're a business owner. See how you might respond to the following question: Does your organization regularly conduct strategic planning sessions culminating in a strategic plan document? Yes or no?

It has been my experience with the thousands of business owners I have spoken to that the vast majority with $10 million in revenue or less respond "no." When I say vast majority, I mean somewhere around 90 percent, give or take 5 percent based on industry, geography, and so on. My informal poll isn't scientific, but the results are overwhelming and consistent.

Now, suppose I ask you this question: Do you have a pretty good plan for what your organization is trying to accomplish, or do you just make it up as you go along?

Here, the results shift dramatically. For those same business owners with under $10 million in company revenues, the vast majority will say they have a plan. In this case, I would estimate around 80 percent have told me they have some type of plan. When I probe a little deeper, I often find out that the plan actually exists, albeit in the owner's head. "I got it all right here!" they say with forefinger pointing to temple. If they do have a written plan, the document is usually sitting high on a bookshelf, uncracked since the thing was written three years ago. ("Gosh, has it been that long?")

So, what's the point? The point is that most small business owners *do* have a plan for their businesses, often with pretty sound thinking and direction. However, the way in which the plan manifests itself is not very effective, and it's certainly not systematic. It may serve the owner to an extent, but it does little for the organization as a whole. That's the problem and that's the opportunity.

Where do I weigh in on the debate of planning? In the simplest terms, I believe:

1. It is irrefutable that planning is a good idea for any small business interested in growth.
2. Formalized strategic planning is not the ideal methodology for most small businesses with under $10 million in revenue. After $10 million, it probably is.
3. Having an effective growth planning system is the best indicator of whether your company *will* grow.
4. Planning for growth is an ongoing process, not an event. It's a never-ending journey, not a destination.

WHAT HAVE I GOT AGAINST STRATEGIC PLANNING?

Nothing, really. Given that most small businesses do very little with regard to planning, a formalized strategic planning process is certainly a far better path to take than doing nothing at all. I mean that sincerely. I would much prefer that my clients immerse themselves in the strict methodology of someone else's strategic planning system than to simply fly by the seat of their pants.

I also believe that implementing the popular notion of a strategic planning system isn't ideal for most privately held, principal-owned small businesses. It's not so much that there's anything wrong with such a system; it's more that people just don't seem to like it. And perceptions are reality. Let's see if you agree.

While there isn't a standard boilerplate for what the strategic plan includes, I think you are familiar with the most common trappings:

- Mission statement
- Vision statement

- Strengths, Weaknesses, Opportunities, and Threats (SWOT) analysis
- Competitive analysis
- Core competencies
- Goals and objectives
- Strategies and tactics

What is a mission? A vision? What's the difference? Does anyone really care? The battle over semantics in most strategic planning efforts gets in the way of real breakthrough thinking. I have seen countless well-intentioned efforts stall in a battle over definitions. That's crazy:

> *A mission statement is defined as "a long awkward sentence that demonstrates management's inability to think clearly." All good companies have one.*
>
> —Scott Adams, 1996, *The Dilbert Principle*

Are you familiar with the cartoon strip Dilbert? In the 1980s, creator Scott Adams tapped into the American office worker's psyche, beginning by pointing out the dehumanizing management style of corporate America. Worker drones, hanging on in quiet desperation in their cubicles, hope to survive one more day in a world of senseless corporate bureaucracy and mind-numbing doublespeak. What makes it so funny is the truth in it all. For a real chuckle, check out Dilbert's online mission statement generator at http://www.dilbert.com/comics /dilbert/games/career/bin/ms.cgi.

Strategic planning doesn't work for many management teams simply because the terminology surrounding the process has become trivial sounding. That's especially true for smaller businesses. Those people who matriculate toward either establishing, or working for, a small business tend to be

Mad Method

I began my career in the rough-and-tumble world of a large Chicago advertising agency. There, when asked to develop an advertising campaign, we usually divided the planning process into three distinct phases.

The first phase was characterized by the large amount of time (months, in many cases) everyone spent preparing situational analyses across the many different disciplines and departments within the agency. The competitive landscape was considered, previous introductions were compared and contrasted, focus groups were conducted, and client directives were discussed (and regularly discarded, I might add).

This culminated in the preparation of the permission to believe (PTB) statement. The PTB gave everyone in the organization an idea of what this product/service was and how it was uniquely positioned in the market. *O'Grady's Potato Chips are cut thicker for more potato taste.* That one sentence took away a few months of my life one year. We also tested "for better dipping" and "for a heartier snacking experience."

The second phase began with the meeting held a few weeks before the final client presentation. Participants representing the various departments came to the meeting armed with their PTB statements and some loose ideas generated by their various departments. A brainstorming session ensued, whereby a wide variety of creative/media directions were discussed. Ultimately, a few specific directions were agreed to by the various departments, and everyone went away to create magic.

The third phase usually started at around 10 P.M. the night before the final client presentation, when it became clear that little

(Continued)

had been done and what had been done didn't really work very well. That's when this same representative group of people from the second phase simply threw something together that had little to do with logic or the PTB statement. Adrenaline and fear become your ally; the ticking clock and four-hour-old pizza, your enemy. In this foxhole, junior research staffers are just as likely to come up with the perfect treatment as the most seasoned creative director. Sleep-deprived suits (the derogatory but ubiquitous term for account executives) suddenly become jingle writers.

And here's the amazing thing: This system worked pretty darn well! I personally observed how this antisystem usually generated outstanding solutions to some pretty vexing problems. I'm not suggesting it was the perfect system. However, I did learn something about the method in this madness.

I learned that when you put a bunch of smart people in a room who (1) possess specific knowledge on a subject, (2) represent a wide variety of skill sets, and (3) are scared to death, the results are often surprisingly positive. (I was going to say "synergistic," but that sounds too Dilbertesque.) I also learned that good ideas can come from the most unlikely of sources, especially when you have surrounded yourself with smart people at all levels (see Chapter 8). Finally, I learned that having all the departments involved fostered a pride of ownership that was carried throughout the organization. People could get behind a plan that they had a hand in creating.

of a certain mind-set. In many cases, escaping the illogical bureaucracies and rhetoric of big business is exactly what has brought them all together. Spend two days deciding whether your company *leverages* or *maximizes* its core competencies, and you'll have a revolt on your hands.

However, the primary reason I'm not a proponent of strategic planning for the under $10 million business has to do with unnecessary structure. Forcing a young-at-heart, nimble, innovative, irreverent, enthusiastic small business into a catch-all, disciplined, rule-oriented, boring boilerplate format really doesn't make sense.

It's analogous to my trying to squeeze into my 10-year-old jeans. I can force it, but it takes unnecessary time and effort, causes some pain, and significantly limits my range of motion. More importantly, the lasting memory of discomfort causes me to look for ways to avoid ever doing it again. It might look okay for a time, but it's really not worth the pain in the end.

SO WHAT DO I SUGGEST?

I'm an advocate of a DIY (do-it-yourself) approach to growth planning. In a nutshell, I maintain that an organization like yours will benefit more from building a proprietary system for growth planning, rather than from relying on someone else's construct. Instead of a fill-in-the-blanks assignment, the actual creation of the process brings positive results in and of itself.

"We started to think and talk strategically from the very beginning," says PrintingForLess.com (PFL) founder, Andrew Field. In the beginning, the planning process was pretty simple. Once a month or so, they would order pizza and get together as a group to discuss any and all things. Not much was written down, but pretty clear goals and directions were established. Field and his key managers also met regularly with their outside board of advisors. "The advisory board really helped us keep our focus early on," Field adds. This system carried the fast-growth company up to the point of about 30 employees. "Once we got over 30 employees," says Field, "it was obvious we needed to do something a little more formalized. By this point we had written a few plans for the outside world and that helped us see how a written plan could help us internally as well."

Since mid-2002, the PFL organization has been developing its own quarterly planning system. Meetings with the outside board are scheduled far in advance. These dates prompt plenty of internal activity by department heads, group leaders, and RATS. (At PFL, RATS are a good thing—it's an acronym for "research and technical support.") "Department heads drive this process," says Field. "Peer pressure between managers to make a goal is the ultimate motivator." Field cautions against waiting until these quarterly plan reviews to identify bad news. "I tell everybody in the organization, 'Do what you say you're going to do, or renegotiate.' We don't want any surprises."

Prioritize growth planning every day. Don't just talk about it—get really good at it. Enjoy the success it brings. Then let the Peter Druckers and Tom Peterses of the world come and study how you did it so others can attempt (and most likely fail) to replicate it. Now that's a plan.

THE 10 R'S OF SMALL BUSINESS
GROWTH PLANNING

I also suggest that there are some common traits to a good growth plan. I know, I just told you to avoid confining structure. That's not what I mean. What I do mean is that I've done quite a bit of growth planning over the years, and I've developed some opinions on things you might want to consider when building your growth planning system. I call them the *10 R's of Small Business Growth Planning.*

1. Representative

For any growth plan to succeed, you have to include the entire organization in the process. It can't be the founder's plan or the management team's plan. Some people call this getting buy-in. I call it logical. If I want people to perform at their very best, then it only makes sense to let them have a say in what they plan to achieve and how they plan to go about achieving it. I learned this helpful piece of information early in my career and quite by accident.

2. Research

Knowledge is power—trite, but true, especially in this Information Age economy in which we all live. Synthesize everything you learn from the ongoing efforts recommended in Chapter 4 (Thoroughly Understand the Marketplace) and be sure to include that synthesis in any planning you do.

3. Remote

I highly recommend going offsite for your planning sessions. Finding a conducive environment in which to work is a must. I usually try to find a quiet, secluded banquet room in a quiet, secluded restaurant. For one thing, I'm fond of eating, so it keeps me close to the food. More importantly, it usually doesn't cost anything for the room if you make it a regular date. Free is good.

Once you get a bit of success and can afford it, going out of town for a night is a good idea. Go just far enough so there is a need to spend the night. It's amazing how much your brain can handle when you fill it up with information and ideas the first afternoon, give it time to digest things overnight, and then set it on problem-solving mode the next morning.

Whatever you do, don't hold a planning session in your office or place of business. There are simply too many distractions. The same holds true for your house. One more suggestion: no alcohol—not just during the actual meeting times, but even that night after the day's work is done. I'm

An Attachment to Team

When I left the advertising business, I took the reins of a small uniform apparel company. I literally went from Michigan Avenue to Main Street, U.S.A., and I carried my small bag of tricks with me. You can probably imagine the looks on the faces of my veteran crew of sewing machine operators when I told them they were going to be involved in a planning session. I asked them to vote for the two representatives who would be their eyes, ears, and voice in the process. I did the same with the office staff. We had only about 15 employees at this point and a "growth planning team" of five.

Our first attempt didn't go too well. I spent too much time trying to educate them on what I knew and not enough listening to what they knew. The second meeting fared little better. They were uncomfortable and shy. I was the proverbial elephant in a china shop. By the end of the first year, we had agreed to little and had implemented even less. I was beginning to question my representative form of growth planning. Maybe it would be easier for me to be the benevolent dictator and just hand out the plan to everyone.

Just when I was about to give up, something pretty amazing happened. In our previous meeting, we had set a goal of increasing our overall production efficiency by an ambitious but achievable percentage by year's end. Now, one of the team members representing the sewing machine operators was coming to the meeting with a new idea. "Some of the women on the machines thought we might be able to find a customized binding attachment that will speed things up," she explained. You probably don't know what a binding attachment is. Honestly, neither did I

(Continued)

(Continued)

at the time. That isn't the point. The point is, she had conveyed our growth goal to her department, listened to their ideas on how to achieve it, investigated a few suppliers of custom attachments, and then speculated about how much we could increase production on two of our best-selling products if we made the change. She had even roughed out a payback of less than one year.

This opened the floodgates. From that point on, the growth team began to think about how they could get into the game of growth. Within two years, we were pretty good at basic planning. We started to see some results. By year five, planning was one of our primary advantages as an organization. Sales had increased by more than 900 percent over the same period—during a significant recession.

Giving everyone in the organization a voice in the growth was one of our most important secrets to success.

no teetotaler, and I could argue that a drink or two might help the creative juices flow. However, it has been my experience that serving alcohol eventually causes problems. You and your team are there to work. Alcohol just gets in the way of the job at hand.

4. Realistic

My grandfather used to quote the Scottish national poet Robert Burns's (1759–1796) famous line: "O would some power the gift give us to see ourselves as others see us." ("To a Louse," verse 8.) It's so true. Organizations, like people, have a very tough time being truthful with themselves. I have heard many small businesses express wide gaps between who they think they are and who they are in reality. Sometimes the gap lies between the owner and the team. Other times it's between departments. Most often I see it between the "new" management team and the old guard.

Any plan that seeks to be a road map for growth must include a realistic assessment of who we are now, where we want to be, how we plan to get there, and the resources we'll need to make the journey successfully. To that end, I advise including at least one outside observer as a reality monitor. A retired business school professor or successful business owner with some time can be used to sniff out the bull from the believable.

I made effective use of a three-person advisory board. It worked very well for me, but I've also seen things work just as well with a skilled facilitator. I don't have a strong recommendation for how you should proceed on this. However, I do like what my friend Chris DiCenso, president of Growth Strategies Partners, has to say on the subject:

> An experienced outside facilitator will provide a streamlined planning process and disciplined focus, challenge "sacred" beliefs, and ensure that all team members provide input to the plan. Unless one of the team members has significant experience developing business strategies, the company will achieve a much better plan with a facilitator.

Chris has helped scores of small businesses in this process, and I respect his views immensely.

5. Results Oriented

The best growth plans are filled with very specific results that stem from a logical interpretation of the current situation and the likely opportunities. To grow the overall business by 25 percent is specific. To increase trial of our new products and services among our targeted prospects and customers from 22 percent to 46 percent by November of next year is even more specific. The more specific you can be now, the better able you are to measure your performance throughout the life of the plan.

I also like having a quantitative way to keep score, as much for morale as for results. Good people seem to like to "make" whatever number you put in front of them. It's engaging. It's challenging. It's motivating.

6. Responsibilities

Who is going to do what? When are they going to do it? The smaller the organization, the better able the team is to isolate responsibilities. Betty is going to do this and Bob is going to do that before our next planning session. It's simple to assign and simple to monitor.

As you grow, however, things become decidedly more difficult. Betty's department will be responsible for this just as soon as she fills the two new positions that have opened up, thanks to our most recent growth spurt. Bob is now in charge of R&D instead of manufacturing, but his old department will be responsible for this and that, while Bob will keep some of this, too, because he's the only one who knows how to do it. Bob's replacement is too new to be held responsible for much beyond getting his business cards printed.

While it will undoubtedly be a challenge, resist the temptation to list all the things you wish you could accomplish in a perfect world. If no one has responsibility for a task, you can count on it not getting done anyway. Don't set yourself up for failure. Don't put it into the plan until you have someone who can own it.

7. (w)Ritten

Any growth plan should be written down if you expect it to have a lasting impact. When it is written down, the plan takes on the sort of permanence that you need. It can be easily shared with others. Drafts, redos, and improvements can be made over time. Remember, the growth plan is a never-ending process, not an event with a start and stop date.

As I suggested before, most small businesses do have some semblance of a plan. Too often, this means the plan is in the owner's head, passed on to the next level of management by word-of-mouth on a need-to-know basis. Like the old children's game of "telephone," by the time the directive reaches someone who actually needs it to do his or her job, the message has often become hopelessly garbled.

Did you ever see the classic screwball movie *Caddyshack?* In it, the executive director of the golf club gives specific instructions to the head greenskeeper to "kill all the gophers." By the time the instructions reach Bill Murray's character, he's understood that he is to "kill all the golfers." The situation is not only hilarious, but also should be familiar to any manager who relies on the spoken word to communicate important information and directions.

The act of writing down notes from the meeting is also imperative. Always assign a nonparticipating scribe. I've seen some groups rotate the responsibility among the regular participants. More often than not, there is one person best suited to the role who should take on the task each time.

I once sat in on a planning session that was taped, to be transcribed later into a written format. There was a malfunction, and the entire session was lost. All subsequent attempts over the next few days to re-create even the most general of discussions and decisions were useless. Even when someone would remember something important, someone else would disagree with the conclusion, if not the entire subject. Understand that I have no problem with recording your sessions, given that the technology works. That's not my point. The point is that things you think you could never forget are often lost when it isn't written down.

Here's my final thought on writing a plan down. *It's also the most important: 15 pages maximum.* It is much easier to write a 50-page tome than it is to codify all your knowledge and thinking and dreams down to their pithy essentials. Scholars disagree on who said, "I would have written you a shorter letter, but I didn't have time." (I've seen attributions to Pearl Buck, Mark Twain, and Marcel Proust, to name but a few. My guess is they all said it at one time or another.) Regardless of who said it, the sentiment pertains to any written document. Err on the side of being concise. In doing so, you make your plan more direct, easier to read, easier to update, and, therefore, stronger.

8. *Repeated*

Once all those involved are more or less nodding their heads yes to the growth plan, it then becomes important to share that information with the organization in all forms of communication. First, get a copy of the plan into everyone's hands. From this point forward, every ad hoc meeting by every division should review the current plan. Every internal newsletter or memo can highlight aspects of the plan. Your web site can also include plan information, with sensitive data password protected in an intranet application. Even new hires should be brought up to speed right away.

The longer you wait to communicate the growth plan, the more it becomes *their* plan versus *our* plan. For some reason, there is a tendency to lose momentum after the arduous task of writing the plan is completed for the first time. Warning: Don't. To push this onto the back burner is a mistake. Remember: *Regularly repeating the plan is a big part of the plan.* Get the word out fast and frequently.

9. Real-Time Monitoring

You've probably heard of Peter Senge's work (*The 5th Discipline: The Art and Practice of the Learning Organization,* 1st edition. New York: Currency Doubleday, 1994) even if you've never heard his name. His breakthrough thinking at MIT's Sloan School of Management in the late 1980s proposed the *systems thinking* method to help a business become a "learning organization" and to "expand the ability to produce." Suffice it to say that Senge was named "Strategist of the Century" by the *Journal of Business Strategy*. That would make Senge the Michael Jordan of Strategy.

One key element of Senge's systems thinking is the important role of delay: "interruptions in the flow of influence which make the consequences of an action occur." The best way I know to describe delay in this context is to imagine someone steering a boat in water for the first time. The time between the turning of the wheel and the resulting change of direction is delay. Usually, a first timer experiences wild fluctuations in direction, as he or she continually misjudges and overcompensates due to the lack of timely feedback. Delay causes the system to function inefficiently.

The same phenomenon can be observed in our business systems, too. I've seen many small business owners and managers blindsided by their end-of-year profit and loss statements. More often than not, the executives don't even see this information until well into the next quarter or even next year. They not only are unable to take corrective action in a timely fashion but also often overcompensate, trying to make up for lost time. This only serves to further exacerbate the overall problem. See if any of this sounds familiar: "I want you to cut the entire advertising budget today!" "Close that office!" Or, "Fire everybody in the sales department now!" It doesn't have to be this way.

Technology and expertise allow us to better monitor our plans in real time. I honestly believe we are now to the point where anyone should be able to push a button and get an accurate view of where they are versus a plan on anything that really matters. Let me say it again . . . anyone in the organization being able to access an accurate picture of the plan and your progress against that plan at any time, accurate to the moment. Why not? Technology can do it. The real question is: Can your people do it? Better yet, can you help them see why it's in their best interest to do it?

At the very least, you should have one piece of paper that gets spit out in an automated way every day and is posted for all to see. How did we do yesterday versus the plan, and how do we stack up for the month, the quarter, and the year?

10. *Regularly Updated*

On September 12, 2001, I, like most Americans, was too traumatized to work. On September 13, I started making calls to my best clients asking how soon we could get together to revisit the growth plan. Some replied, "How soon can you get here?" Others were perplexed by the question. "How can we plan at a time like this? Besides, we don't do our planning until November."

Planning (especially making changes to the existing plan) is most appropriate during times of flux. Big changes to the environment in which you do business might mean big changes to the growth plan. That seems pretty irrefutable to me. I also don't believe in initiating the process at an arbitrary starting point. Most successful growth companies plan when it's needed. In the software business, that might be every month. In the packaged salt business, it's probably less often.

Defining how often to evaluate your progress as a team is one of the most important decisions you'll make as a growth leader. Pay close attention to your specific circumstances, adopting a schedule uniquely appropriate to your organization. There is a right answer on this; however, it differs for everyone.

SUGGESTED NEXT STEPS

1. Start creating your own growth planning system by tapping representatives from throughout the organization who will participate.

2. Kick off the planning with an off-site meeting.

3. Identify an outside observer (or observers) who can consistently participate in your growth planning.

4. Be sure your plan is written, well communicated, and updated on a regular basis.

5. Keep your plan to 15 pages maximum.

6

RULE 4:
DEVELOP CUSTOMER-
DRIVEN PROCESSES

If you can't describe what you are doing as a process, you don't know what you're doing.

—W. Edwards Deming

Is your organization customer driven? Every time I ask this question of small business owners, I get the same answer: an emphatic *Yes!* They always say yes. But do their customers agree? My experiences suggest that, in most cases, the customers probably don't.

Many business owners confuse being customer driven with "giving good service." If the goods ship out on time or if a service is delivered efficiently, they pat themselves on the back for a job well done. A year later the customer goes somewhere else, and the owner has no idea why.

Most companies hear this advice and apply it to their internal structure, and those things—for example, standard operating procedures, financial management systems, and purchasing standards—are important. However, too often companies develop their processes based on limited information. The voice of the customer is muffled or completely silent. Growth companies don't make this mistake.

Define everything that you do from a customer's perspective, and then look for ways to improve that every single day. Find out what customers *really* want you to concentrate on; then do those things better than anyone else. Don't just satisfy your customers. Anticipate their needs to the point where they are recommending you to everyone they know.

WHO OWNS THE INVOICE?

Perhaps you read the last section and think that you are the rare exception. You are saying to yourself, "Steve's right; most companies aren't customer driven. Thank goodness we have stressed a customer-driven orientation so much in my organization."

Let me see if I can't convince you that you probably have more work to do.

Let's take a look at something as simple as your invoices. Not every organization invoices customers, but most do. (If you are a retailer, your receipt is analogous to the invoice. Some of this won't apply exactly to you, but I think you'll get the gist.) Few processes are as common to all businesses as the mundane invoice, yet consider how *un*customer driven the invoice is for most companies.

When do you send your customers an invoice? How do you send your customers an invoice? What do your invoices look like? What are the terms? Most importantly, who determines what information is printed on that invoice? Who determines when it goes out, how it is sent, and even why it is sent?

If you are truly customer driven, it is your customer who should decide these things. In most companies I've observed, the last person who should have this responsibility is somehow the one who has been selected: Carl, the company comptroller; Olivia, the office manager; or Betty, the bulldog of accounts receivable. The absolute worst is companies that allow the computer guy to decide how the invoices should work. These people all tend to focus on the internal. When left to their own devices, they build processes that are company friendly. The invoices are easy to administer, standardized for internal benefit, and able to be batched and disseminated on a fixed schedule. By nature, these team members are not customer focused. They are task focused. Unless you have a training or incentive program that changes their focus, they are not concentrating on eking out extra sales or continually increasing customer retention.

To be truly customer driven, any process that "touches" a customer needs to fully integrate the best thinking of your entire organization. Something as seemingly simple as an invoice can be markedly improved with a slightly different perspective. Pulling together your marketing, quality control, sales staff, shipping department, and customer service people is the best way I know to build a truly customer-friendly invoice. If you are a professional services firm (e.g., a law firm), I would include everyone from paralegals to administrative assistants to senior partners. I know some of you don't have all these formal departments or titles yet, so I suggest you put on those various hats to see invoicing from a different perspective. For instance, "I have on my marketing hat now. How would a marketing person look at this invoice with a customer in mind?" Now I have my quality control hat on. "How would a quality control expert reinvent this invoice with the customer in mind?"

Once you have brought together all the best thinking in your organization, you will find that developing a customer focus in your invoicing process will become much easier. If the payment terms your customers need to do business with you don't fit your standard terms, you change them. In fact, I don't know why anyone even has standard terms. If your customer wants to pay you with terms of "net 60," then that's *their* standard terms. They decide the terms and you price accordingly. You need to meet them or somebody else will. Most organizations I work with see terms as a financial and accounting decision. In reality, terms are primarily a pricing issue. Pricing is a marketing issue. Therefore, if anyone should be making a decision on terms, it should be a marketing type.

If an invoice should be e-mailed instead of faxed, with a detailed listing of everything customers bought, do it. If it should go out on the second Tuesday of the month instead of the fourth Friday, make it happen. If customers need their purchase order number, the purchasing person's name, and your salesperson's name and phone number all on the invoice, you do that as well. With today's technology, none of this should be all that difficult.

When a customer of your company calls to express a problem with an invoice or to get more information, does a pleasant and accommodating person on the other end of the phone take care of it? Or does your customer have to argue with Betty the Bulldog? If you're doing it right, the person on the phone resolves the invoicing issue to the customer's satisfaction quickly and efficiently, whether the details fall under his or her job description or not. In the truly customer-driven organization, the person who took the call knows to bring the issue to someone's attention. Customer feedback continually hones the process.

What's my point? The vast majority of companies treat their invoices as sacred. They print internal gobbledygook on cheaply produced, hard-to-read invoices that mean little to the customer. How many invoices have you seen with a string of internal accounting numbers on them and then something like, "You owe me $10,000 within 15 days"? Many companies then employ surly accounts receivable people who can't or won't explain what all those numeric codes mean. They often guard your money more jealously than you ever would and seemingly view most customers as the enemy.

I'm not telling you to roll over and get meek when customers are late on their bills. I'm not advising you to let people take advantage of you. I talk later about customers who are more trouble than they are worth. However, I do advise that you do everything in your power to make sure you don't put obstacles in the path of the customers you value. My point is not specifically about invoicing. Invoicing is just one of potentially thousands of ways in which your organization can truly develop customer-driven processes. *That's* my point.

A NOTE ON PROCESSES

There are so many types of businesses: product based, service based; business to consumer, business to business; bigger, smaller; urban, rural; capital-equipment intensive, people intensive. Therefore, it is sometimes difficult to generalize about processes, which, as a speaker to business owners, is one of my greatest challenges. Invoicing hits a pretty wide swath. So does my Milkshake Story.

There is one process that is universal to every growth business. The only way I've seen to grow a business is to improve the processes surrounding your ability to acquire and retain customers. I have not come across one growth company that doesn't excel at this. Conversely, when I am brought in to help stagnant or struggling small businesses, invariably, their problems stem from their inability to master this process.

The Milkshake Story

As a professional speaker and consultant, I'm on the road a lot. I average about 100 nights a year in hotels. There are many aspects of business travel that can wear you down, but I try to keep a smile on my face at all times. One way I do that is by keeping my eye on the prize. To get through a trying day of planes, trains, and automobiles, I keep looking forward to something that will reward me at the end of the day.

Recently, I checked into a big chain, business-oriented hotel. On entering the room, I immediately went to the phone to call room service. My prize was going to be a vanilla milkshake. I had been thinking about it all day and could almost taste it.

"Good evening, Mr. Little, this is Stuart in room service. How may I help you?" a pleasant voice answered.

"Hello, Stuart, I'd like a vanilla milkshake, please," I replied.

"I'm sorry, Mr. Little, but we don't have milkshakes," Stuart said. I was crushed.

After thinking for a moment, I said. "All right, Stuart, tell me this: Do you have any vanilla ice cream?"

"Yes, of course!" he responded enthusiastically.

"Okay, do you have any milk?" I then asked.

"Yes, we have milk," he replied.

"All right, Stuart, here's what I would like you to do. Please send up a tray with a bowl of vanilla ice cream, half a glass of milk, and a long spoon. Could you do that for me, please?"

"Certainly, right away, sir," Stuart replied.

I hung up the phone, and five minutes later there was a knock on the door. Sure enough, there on the tray was a bowl of vanilla ice cream, half a glass of milk, and a long spoon—all the

(Continued)

ingredients you need for a vanilla milkshake. But, of course, they don't have vanilla milkshakes.

Now, my question to you is this: Is Stuart stupid? Perhaps, but I don't think so. I don't think he's stupid, because this isn't the first time this scenario has played out for me. In fact, I've probably repeated this exercise more than 100 times over the past five years. In only 20 percent of the cases have I received a milkshake.

So no, I don't think it's the individual that is stupid. It's the systems that are stupid. The primary obstacle is that milkshakes are not on the menu, and there is no key code for milkshakes on their point-of-sale touch screens. Therefore, they do not exist. Some hotels are now offering smoothies on their room service menu, which tells me the second most common obstacle, lack of a blender in the kitchen, isn't even an issue.

I feel sorry for these big name business hotels. In an effort to be outstanding, they feel forced to invest in standardization. They spend a fortune crunching data on their customers to come up with "meaningful profiles" that mean nothing. Think of the billions they spend each year trying to train their staffs how to make me happy (because, believe me, I am the target). Despite all this effort, they often fail miserably in giving customers what they really want. The people who work there may be smart. They may even sincerely try their best to make each customer satisfied. But they are hampered by stupid systems.

Here's the lesson of the milkshake story. Don't allow your systems to make your organization stupid. Find ways to build flexible operating procedures so those best and brightest people you hired can do their jobs. Don't make them have to be a systems analyst to input a special order that's "off the menu." Don't make them shut down a whole shipping department to send a package

(Continued)

> *(Continued)*
>
> to Canada. Don't make your best sales rep jump through hoops sending triplicate forms to accounting because she had to give your biggest customer slightly different payment terms. And if you run a hotel, find a way to keep room service from resorting to a bowl of ice cream, half a glass of milk, and a spoon when all the guest really wanted was a milkshake.

THE 10 T'S OF CUSTOMER ACQUISITION AND RETENTION

Trying to grasp all the factors that determine whether a customer buys from you and keeps buying from you can be overwhelming. That's why I've developed the 10 T's of Customer Acquisition and Retention. These are the most important elements for any organization interested in improving in this area.

1. Training

Do your new hires know what makes you tick? Do they know why you exist and what matters to your customers? The training I'm talking about is customer-driven training, not internally driven training. Most small businesses have some rudimentary form of initial training, but it is focused on how to work the cash register, how to input data into the computer, or how to file the paperwork. Yes, those things are necessary to learn, but they come with time. Most of that kind of training has little to do with what really matters from a customer standpoint. The answers to the following questions are what effective employees *really* need to be trained about:

- Why do people buy from us?
- What do we do differently from everyone else?

- Why do people buy from us and not the other guys?
- When people buy from the other guys, why do they do it?
- What makes us unique?
- What do our customers care the most about?
- What are the primary tasks you need to know, and how do those tasks relate to the customers' needs?

When you can answer these questions and train people on those topics, you will have a powerful training program. You assume that customer satisfaction is obvious, but it is not. (See the Oyster Bar Story.) Most new employees have no idea what satisfies a customer of your company. You need to teach them.

Dedicate some serious time to the training that really delivers. Each new employee should go through at least one day dedicated to an orientation to the company, its values, and its history. The best growing companies pull in the company founders, the top sales reps, or the president to explain the company's core reason for being. They get new hires up to speed on how the company is different, what it does better, and why it is going to grow.

I have observed on more than one occasion the training process of new hires at PrintingForLess.com (PFL). While PrintingForLess.com can point to many competitive advantages, its four-month-long training process for new hires is, in my opinion, the most important. Everyone, from a back-of-house pressman to the newest technical service representative, is fully indoctrinated into the "customer-centric mind-set" that is PFL. In many cases, people being trained come from a printing background. That's fine. They may have a slight headstart relative to their fellow trainees. But the customer-driven processes at PFL are unique, so even the most seasoned print industry veteran will need every bit of the four months of

The Oyster Bar Story

For many years my family and I have lived in sunny Wilmington, North Carolina, in an area called Wrightsville Beach. About 10 months out of the year, it's the perfect place to live. In July and August, however, our beach becomes overrun with tourists. Therefore, on the weekends, we often drive to another beach area we've come to love. This area is not only less touristy but also offers a plethora of great seafood restaurants.

For years, our favorite seafood could be found at a shabby-chic oyster bar that boasted of "oysters as big as your fist." The oysters were good, but that wasn't why we picked this particular place. The staff, composed mostly of would-be professional surfers, out-of-work actresses, and assorted beach bums, was friendly and a lot of fun. We always had a good time when we went out to eat there. Apparently so did a lot of other people, because the business was successful and the owner started looking at expansion.

What the owner decided to do, however, was not just do what he was currently doing in a bigger way. He decided to bring in restaurant consultants who had worked with big chain restaurants: the likes of Applebee's, Bennigan's, and Chili's. These consultants told him what kind of point of sale system to buy, told him the best way to hire and train employees, and showed him how to turn more tables by running his operation more efficiently.

We went back to his oyster bar after all these changes had taken place. There were no flaky part-time actresses and beach bums waiting on us. Instead, we were served by an efficient, well-groomed young man who did all the right things in the right

(Continued)

order. However, he rarely smiled, and he never made eye contact. When he said, "You have everything you need—right?" it was more a statement than a question. The place was quieter, there wasn't as much laughter, and it didn't feel the same. It felt like a big chain restaurant.

That waiter probably thought he was doing a bang-up job. He didn't forget anything, the orders arrived quickly, and he "turned" his tables because people didn't stick around too long. The owner probably thought things were going fine because everything was running efficiently. I don't doubt that the oysters themselves were receiving high marks on the newly implemented customer satisfaction survey.

What the owner forgot, however, was that it wasn't about the oysters. We could get oysters anywhere. Every bait shop and roadside stand had them for sale. I could even scoop them up from the end of my backyard on the intracoastal waterway and grill them myself. The reason we went there, and most other people went there, was for the *experience*. The place had personality, the people had personality, and it was fun. We haven't gone back, and from an informal sample of friends and neighbors, I know we're not alone. The business is now undoubtedly contracting, and they're probably blaming the economy or people undercutting them on price. Sadly, they somehow lost the knack for knowing what people really bought from them. I heard they are now trying to sell the business and not having much luck.

Are you focused on what your customers really care about, or are you focused on what you internally think is important?

Here's the point of the Oyster Bar Story. It's not about the oysters; it's about the customer experience. Determine what you are really selling, and then make that experience better than anyone else's.

hands-on training to deliver at the peak performance level expected by colleagues and customers alike.

Historically, small business has had the reputation of not offering strong training. I'm not sure that this reputation is always valid. When it is valid, it is usually because small businesses think they can't afford it. However, I am sure that the majority of small businesses can't afford *not* to do this kind of training.

2. Touches

Every time you come in contact with a customer, it's a "touch" and an opportunity to shine.

I worked as president of a company making apparel with corporate logos. Our competition saw touches in two places: the initial marketing communications and the first phone call. We went beyond that to put effort into the art department, the sample department, and the shipping processes—even down to something as detailed as the packing slip—because when we got the order, that was just the first step. In the world of apparel, people return things, even if you do everything perfectly. The personal touches—how we handled the two returns out of 42 shipped—was how we won over the customer and got more business. We took what the customer perceived to be a potentially negative experience and turned it into a big positive. Removing the proverbial thorn in the lion's paw allowed us to move beyond simple satisfaction. We were building lifetime loyalty and value.

What is far more common, especially with the big companies you are competing with, is the dropped ball, the wasted opportunity, or the negative that gets even more negative. We all have far too many examples of these in our heads, but here are two examples of customer touches that the company should have had complete control of, both related to outbound correspondence.

Like most people, I'm always looking for a good deal when I travel. One airline I fly most of the time does a pretty good job in some areas and a lousy job in others. Every week I get an e-mail from them with a host of special deals and offers. Invariably, when I call the reservations number to book a flight, they know nothing about the deal I just received in my inbox. The right hand and left hand are in different worlds. Here's a marketing department sending me a message each week, which I've actually taken the time to open, yet they can't service me in the simple way I want to do business—over the phone. Sometimes I get an e-mail from this airline that will prompt me to pick up the phone and place an order. The first thing their automated system requires is that I enter my frequent flyer number. Then they know who I am. A customer service representative then asks me for my e-mail address so he or she can send a confirmation. Now keep in mind I have flown more than one million miles with this airline in just the past 10 years and have received literally hundreds of e-mails from them. How is it possible that their system cannot link their outbound marketing database with their customer service database?

Here's another example. When I travel, I'm generally flying to one of a handful of specific airports. More than half of my speaking engagements are in the big conference and convention cities: Orlando, Las Vegas, New Orleans, Atlanta, and Chicago. Some of the online travel agencies offer a free service that will alert me by e-mail when the lowest fare falls below a certain price that I determine. Recently, I was happy to see one of the fares drop way below the threshold, so I clicked on the link. Instead of a screen offering me a way to buy tickets, I got a blank screen with this message:

HTTP ERROR: 403 Forbidden
Directory access not allowed

I'm no techie, but it was obvious somebody inserted a dead link of some kind in the e-mail, and whoever is supposed to check these things went home early or didn't do his or her job. Regardless, here was a point of customer contact that could have resulted in a sale of three tickets immediately and maybe a hotel and rental car on top of it. Instead, the company blew it. Their home page address wasn't in the e-mail, so I clicked on a rival's site I had bookmarked. The company who had sent me this prime information lost the sale and probably countless others because the customers' experience wasn't handled properly. The scary thing is that they'll never know how much money they lost that day because most of their customers won't say anything. I certainly didn't. Most people just bought from somebody else that day and thought a little bit less of that company forever.

Every contact with the customer is important—and can have a direct impact on your customer acquisition and retention. This includes the initial phone call, credit terms, confirming e-mail, returns—everything that your customer sees and hears from your organization. Remember, finding and keeping customers is a *touchy* subject.

3. Total View

As it relates to customers, everyone in your organization should be able to access everything they need to know, anytime or anywhere. This is difficult, yes, but not impossible.

How many times have you heard, "that's not my department" or "that's not my job"? That's a pitiful response, and if anyone in your company says that, you should be embarrassed. He or she is costing you money and stifling your growth.

There are plenty of reasons this attitude surfaces. Maybe your employees don't personally have the technical knowledge to address the request. Maybe there are too many territorial disputes in your organization. Maybe that particular person is just plain lazy. You need to fix these problems, either through better training, better people, or better technology—probably all of these. The problem of inadequate technical knowledge is one of the easiest problems to address. Technology allows you to solve problems seamlessly, without ever showing what steps got you there.

How many times does it look like the right hand doesn't know what the left hand is doing in your organization? See if any of these look familiar:

- Have you ever sent out marketing materials to people who are on credit hold?
- Have you ever invoiced people with standard terms after they've negotiated custom terms with your sales organization?
- Have you mailed out brochures to people who haven't worked at that company for two years?
- Has your marketing department advertised services that the sales department says nobody wants to buy?
- Has your shipping department sent packing slips that bear no resemblance to the customer's invoice or sales contract?
- Have your people answering the phones been clueless about what your customers have ordered and what offers you have sent them by e-mail?
- Have customers ever tried in vain to return a product that they purchased online to your physical location?

To grow your business, you need a total view. You need to make sure anyone who interacts with customers in any way has a total view or at least knows where to go to get the answers in a hurry. Through training and our next T, technology, you can make it happen.

4. *Technology*

This book has a whole chapter on technology, but here I talk about technology that impacts your customers. Technology is making it increasingly easier to gather, store, and interpret information about our customers.

It has become popular in recent years to put in customer relationship management (CRM) systems. U.S. companies have spent billions to set up formal CRM software systems. This software allows companies to determine which customers have spent the most, get a view of customers' past transactions when they call, and route them to the person who can serve them best. When it all works as advertised, a CRM system can be a powerful tool. But much of the time it doesn't, as we have all experienced when calling a big company's customer service department.

That kind of CRM can cost a fortune. But remember, you have some kind of CRM system in place now, whether it is in file folders or an in-house database. Don't confuse a software solution with the important function we all share—managing the customer base. Improving true CRM, especially for a small company, can be what makes or breaks the business.

Simply put, technology can improve your customers' experience. I'm not saying make your company robotic. Technology can make your organization more responsive and more humanistic by allowing your people to do their jobs better. Technology can free up your people's time so they can handle the things that human beings do best.

Too often, small business owners believe that their customers always want to talk to them. That's not true. What is true is that we've trained our customers that talking to us in real time, by phone or face to face, is how you get things done. When I speak about automating mundane tasks, many business owners think I am advocating a soulless, mechanized customer encounter. Far from it—the idea here is to provide a higher level of service in those areas where technology is the best tool.

When I was president of that corporate apparel company, 40 percent of the time our customer service staff spent on the phone with customers was answering two questions: "Is my order close to shipping?" and "Can I get another catalog?" By simply automating these two mundane, repetitive tasks via our Web interface, our highly trained customer service staff was able to become increasingly proactive, not reactive, and provide more high-value service. Computer systems don't do a good job of answering questions such as, "How red are your red shirts?" They can't answer questions such as, "Bob gained a lot of weight since last year's show; do you think he needs an XXL or a 3XL?" These types of questions present an opportunity to really shine. Our well-trained staff could now devote their newfound time to answering these more qualitative questions. By freeing up our staff's time, technology allowed us to provide more quality touches.

Most business owners agree that face-to-face contact is the most valuable contact you can have with a client or customer. I agree. Nothing is more valuable than face-to-face contact in any business. According to Cahners Research, the cost of the average face-to-face sales call was $329 in 2001. It is a tremendously valuable tool that should be used properly. Due to the high cost of face-to-face communications, we've found other ways to communicate with our customers, and there has always been a relationship between the cost and the value.

We have the telephone, which is a very effective tool. While not nearly as valuable as face-to-face contact, it is still a tremendous tool for certain applications. The telephone has an auditory component, a real-time component, and a two-way interaction component that makes it extremely valuable. Everyone has it, and we can all use it. However, while it is significantly less effective than face-to-face contact, the telephone is still an expensive tool. If you factor in all of your real costs, from telephony hardware to health insurance, the average outbound sales call your company makes can cost anywhere from $15 to $35. Taking an inbound order from a customer can cost you an average of $7 to $12.

Mail is also an effective tool in the right circumstances. Most businesses still mail invoices. They still mail catalogs. Many companies still use mail to distribute compelling offers. Compared to real-time, two-way communication, mail seems limited, but the corresponding costs still make it a good value. Fax is cheaper still, but the limitations of color and format reduce its value.

With e-mail, for the first time ever, we have a touch tool that does not obey the laws of previous business communication techniques. With e-mail, there is no correlation between the cost of a contact and the value of that contact. While the cost of all your communication options continues to increase, the value of e-mail communication continues to increase. (Some of you are thinking, "Hey, my long-distance bill has dropped in half in the past five years." But remember, it's people on the phone that really cost you money. Why do you think big business is outsourcing their call centers to places like India and the Philippines?)

Let's say your company sends a promotional e-mail introducing your latest product or service to 100 random, existing customers already on your e-mail list. It goes well. Technology now allows you to expand that effort with confidence at relatively little additional cost. If you want to send the same offer to all 20,000 of your customers the next day, there is no real incremental increase in costs. And the future of e-mail will offer an even more valuable contact. Imagine your bright, smiling face yipping and yapping in your customer's inbox (for those who request it, anyway), describing your daily specials or latest innovations. E-mail will have an auditory component and a visual component close to real time, at a cost below that of a fax on a per-contact basis. That is powerful, amazing, and just around the corner. The same is true of a web site. The incremental cost for 100,000 web site visitors a week rather than 1,000 is next to nothing these days.

This is one of the reasons the Web is still a really big deal. I talk about technology in more detail in Chapter 7, but the bottom line is that the Internet has indeed changed everything. Don't let the dot-com meltdown make you think you can avoid using the Web and e-mail for your business. No matter what business you are in, you have to get good at using these technologies because your customers need for you to be.

5. Tailored

Customer communication is going to look far different in the near future than it does now. The key is going to be honing your database to give all customers what they want, when they want it, the way they want it.

There was a term in vogue in the late 1990s—*mass customization.* The notion was that many successful companies had gone beyond the old paradigm of mass production and had put processes in place to give customers what they need. It centered on Dell building you the computer you wanted when you called or Levi Strauss sending you custom-tailored jeans.

But we're past that now. Now the idea is what my friend and noted direct marketing expert Tracy Emerick calls "mass customerization." The notion of customizing for each customer needs to go beyond mere production. I talked about custom invoices earlier, and this same concept needs to apply to every touch point. It is especially important in terms of marketing communication.

In direct marketing, for example, the main components are the list, the offer, the format/medium, and the copy. Nearly all companies I've worked with spend the bulk of their direct offering time on copy and format. That's the opposite of what they should be doing. Everything comes from the list and the offer. The rest are details. If you are offering the right deal to the right people at the right time, you can deliver it on a napkin or explain it in a two-minute phone call.

In the world of commercial printing, every product delivered has always been mass customized. The good folks at PrintingForLess.com have taken this concept to the next level. A large part of the company's growth can be attributed to the ability to better understand the unique nature of every customer. For instance, when the company first started taking online orders in 1999, they accepted only a few file formats. Now five years later, they accept 42. You can have your order shipped by any method you want, in any time frame that you need. Need your order faster? Not a problem. PrintingForLess.com can accommodate you for a nominal (but very profitable) surcharge.

6. Trenching

Trenching is a term I use to refer to the process of finding actionable information in customer data and using that to grow your business. Some people would call this data mining, but you don't really dig for it and remove it. Instead, you move along a trench looking at the stratification, like a geologist. (Besides, data mining doesn't start with the letter "t," so that would blow my whole premise.) When trenching, you are trying to find answers to the following key questions:

- What kind of customers should we serve?
- What kind of customers do we currently serve?
- How can we describe our best types of customers?
- What patterns can we find in our customers that predict future lifetime value, potential offers, or potential actions?

You can nearly always find patterns in the data: why people buy, when they buy, what they buy, what kind of offers elicit a response. If Tony buys only logo hats from me year after year like clockwork and nothing else, I'm probably wasting money sending him a shirt catalog 12 times a year. If Candlewic president Bill Binder has a customer who buys only soap supplies from him, it wouldn't make sense to continually offer that customer special pricing on candle supplies. Maybe once or twice a year, he would offer special pricing to see if he could elicit a trial, but certainly not as often as he would to his known candle supply buyers.

Who owns your customer data in your organization? If you're like most companies that have gone beyond a few employees, the data are all over the place. Finance owns one chunk, purchasing or shipping owns a chunk, marketing owns another, and sales has different pieces altogether. Many of the salespeople might have half their info scribbled on notes somewhere, and the other departments are each protecting their fiefdom from intruders. You need to figure out who owns all the pieces and pull them together so the data become meaningful. There are software vendors who want to help you with this, some of them quite good. But even the best software is only as good as the legacy data you can input. The data are only as good as the ongoing processes for gathering and sharing that data.

Some people will find this information of great value. Others will say, "Hey, Steve, I just own an ice cream shop. How is trenching data going to help me grow my business?" That's a legitimate question, and here's your answer. How difficult would it be to gather customers' e-mails in exchange for a free sample? Maybe you can even ask for their favorite flavor, too, and get the entire family's birthdays. Every birthday you send out a coupon. If you ever want to send out a survey, you've got your list. You've got the idea.

Who creates information in your organization? There is a big difference between data and information. Fifty lines of customer data is still just data. Information is this: Ellen is the key decision maker, but she asks Joe for input; the company's fiscal budget year starts in July, and they respond best to extended payment terms.

Don't be data rich and information poor. Getting raw data is easy. What you need to get is actionable information. Fifty pages of data is often useless, but one page of actionable information can be gold. Getting information is more difficult, but that's what's going to fatten your bank account.

When you get to the point where you can analyze your data and create real information, you can start making product/service decisions that are based on more than gut instinct. Finding this information takes more expertise but creates more value. You start profiling customers and predicting outcomes. You can expand your business and say, "My models show me that if I spend this amount of money to acquire these people, who have this much lifetime value, I will have this much money at the end of it." That not only allows you to make good spending decisions but also builds information you can take to the bank—literally. Find experts who can make this happen. The companies who really know their customers and know where to find more like them are the ones that will grow.

There's another key advantage to getting good at trenching. If you are finding new customers and serving your good ones well, you can then prune your garden to get rid of the dead-wood. The people who always grill you on price and pay you late are also the ones that complain the most. Anyone who says, "We love all our customers" is probably lying (and not growing). With most companies, the bottom 10 or 20 percent of their customers (in terms of revenue) take up as much as 50 percent of their time. Can you ever really make money on these kinds of customers?

For most business owners, it is very difficult to give up any customer—we all remember a time when we didn't have any. But how much more productive and profitable could you be if you got rid of the marginal customers? How many more good customers with attractive lifetime values could you service instead? If the relationship isn't working, the two of you are probably not a good fit. End the relationship. Let your competitors deal with those customers. Knowing whom you can serve well and whom you can't is critical to becoming a high-growth company. Be selective and give up the time wasters. Your bottom line will improve dramatically.

7. Time Bombs

Any company interested in growth needs to do things cheaper, faster, and better to win business. The only way we can consistently deliver on the "faster" part is to build and plant *time bombs* throughout our organization. Time is of the essence in today's economy. Attention-getting time bombs of some type need to go off whenever you are not doing a good job of managing the customer's expectation of time. The entire organization needs to see, hear, and feel the obvious warning signs of impending time problems.

PrintingForLess.com has set up a system where every order is being tracked at all times. Orders that are close to being in trouble set off an alarm in the company system.

When there is an alarm on this dashboard, the whole place goes nuts trying to figure out what went wrong, how to fix it, and how to keep it from happening again. The project is not late at this point. It's just in danger of getting that way if people don't react. It's a time bomb.

Here's an interesting story on how seriously PrintingForLess .com values the importance of exceeding customer expectations as it relates to time. Every time we get together, everyone in the organization, at one time or another, refers to the company's on-time shipment performance. What percentage of orders were shipped before the promised ship date? What percentage shipped on time? How many times did the company drop the ball last week, last month, or last quarter? These types of measurements of time performance are posted in prominent locations throughout the facility on a daily basis and are on everyone's computer dashboard. The company has identified the crucial role on-time delivery plays in commercial printing.

Here's the funny part. In all this time the employees and managers have been talking about not meeting a promised ship date, I assumed that customers were receiving their printing materials after the date promised. I was wrong. In those rare instances (less than one-half of 1 percent of the time) where the orders were "late," the customer still received the order on the date expected. *Late,* to PrintingForLess.com, means that the company had to pay extra shipping costs on the order to get it there on time, thus eroding the profit margin.

In your organization, how many times do you or other key people find out about a problem after it's too late to really fix it or at a point where it is twice as expensive to fix it as it would have been earlier? The worst is when you hear about a time problem for the first time from your customer. Find a way to warn your organization with time bombs that no one can ignore.

8. *Tractable*

Tractable is defined as: (adj.) susceptible to suggestion; a personality sensitive to other's desires [syn: malleable, responsive].

This isn't a word you hear every day. Being tractable means you are susceptible to suggestion. You are sensitive to other people's desires. To be successful as a growth company in today's economy, you need to be malleable and responsive. Satisfaction is not on a continuum. People don't move along in stages from "completely unsatisfied" to "completely satisfied." By being malleable and responsive, I can grab customers and immediately move them from the bottom of the scale to the top. If I can solve that customer's problem in a way that's far beyond what they were expecting, I've now got a loyal customer. I have that customer's satisfaction and repeat business. Most importantly, I probably have the customer's recommendation to their colleagues, family members, and friends. A potential negative is now a positive.

The best way to accomplish this is to drive decision making down to the point of contact. The person serving the customer needs the power to turn a negative into a positive immediately, with a solution that goes beyond the customer's expectation.

One of the companies that has made this tractability part of its core value system is the Ritz-Carlton hotel company. Here is an example from my experience. My parents live in Amelia Island, Florida, within walking distance of a beautiful Ritz-Carlton. I was not a guest at the hotel; my wife and I had gone there to shoot a game of pool one evening on a Thanksgiving holiday weekend. Some kids were playing pool on the table, even though it was after 9:00 P.M., and they shouldn't have been there, according to the prominently posted rules. Their father was playing with them. Some other guests came in and were unhappy about the kids being there, and unkind words eventually turned into wholly inappropriate language and loud, belligerent behavior.

Here's what happened next: Ritz-Carlton comped all the drinks my wife and I bought that night, before and after the incident, and gave us a free dinner. (Did I mention I wasn't even a guest at the hotel?) Everyone else who had been in the room and witnessed the ugliness got the same treatment: Any of the bystanders who were staying at the hotel had their rooms comped as well. Who made this decision? Not the hotel manager, not the night manager, but the young woman who had been bringing us our drinks. Maybe she was a waitress or maybe she was the bar manager, but it didn't matter. She had the power to say, "This is an ugly and embarrassing situation, but I know I have the power to take this from zero to 100." Instead of a bad experience, all the guests left with smiles on their faces. Now that's a tractable organization!

Please understand that I am not suggesting that you give away the store for free. For many of you, that simply is not economically feasible. I am suggesting that the vast majority of customers simply want to be treated fairly. If things don't go exactly as planned and you are able to rectify a situation *beyond* their expectations, you will win in the long run.

If you gain a reputation for going above and beyond on customer issues and complaints, will there be some cheaters? Sure, you will get a few opportunists and freeloaders. Usually, however, the positive effects of exceeding customer expectations such as increased loyalty and word-of-mouth advertising far outweigh these rare occasions of abuse. A customer who will recommend you to others is the most valuable customer you can get.

At the very least, be sure that you never hear words like these uttered by people in your organization:

- "I'm sorry, but that's our policy."
- "If I do this for you, I'll have to do it for everybody."
- "You'll have to speak to my manager. I don't have the power to do that."
- "I don't know if I'm allowed to do that."
- "If it were up to me, you know I would do it."

9. Telepathy

You and your employees need to have telepathy. You have to be able to anticipate the future. Your organization must assume a proactive stance as it relates to all your customers' needs. You have to foresee any and all potential problems that could crop up before they do crop up. You also need to recognize the patterns that are indicative of future success or failure or future opportunities.

I was in a focus group with business owners where the moderator asked what kind of TV character summed up what their organization is like. What character defined their company's personality? There were some really interesting answers from everyone, with a wide variety of characters from the past few decades—everyone from Mary Tyler Moore to George Jefferson. The best answer I heard was Radar O'Reilly from M*A*S*H. In case you are too young to remember Radar, he had the uncanny knack for understanding what was going to happen before it ever did. He was always in the right place, at the right time, with the right solution for that particular crisis. He continually saved the day, but he always did it in a quiet, unassuming way. He didn't expect to get the credit; he just wanted things to go well. While his loyalties may have been split internally at times, he never wavered from his clear customer focus. The wounded and the maimed were his only priority, and he would do literally anything to improve their condition. To that extent, Radar O'Reilly might be the most customer-driven character in TV history.

You want to have that kind of predictive power in your organization. One of the best ways to do that is to make it easy to communicate with your company, especially to complain. You want your best customers to tell you how they think things are going, even when they are not going well. That tells you what they really want and what they are willing to pay you to do for them. They will give you the best indication of the actions you need to take to improve and grow. As we learned in the Potato Chip Story in Chapter 4, you need to understand your customers better than they understand themselves. Your customers may not know how you can solve their problems, but they can certainly tell you about their points of pain. Find a way to solve those pain points. You then need to find out what they really want but haven't told you yet.

Remember the Milkshake Story earlier in this chapter? How difficult would it be for room service at any one of the leading business travel hotels to call me upon arrival and offer to bring me that vanilla milkshake? Apparently, pretty difficult, as it has never happened to me once, despite having made the request over 100 times in recent years, at no less than 10 well-known chains. Seriously! This isn't some over-the-top request like a champagne bath for my poodle. I'm asking for something that has a total real cost of less than a dollar, and I'm willing to pay pretty much whatever it takes to get it. It is inconceivable to me that their systems are so deaf and have no telepathic abilities. It is my sincere hope that the release of this book will prompt at least one of these national hotel chains to predict this customer's highly predictable needs. (On page xvi you'll find my e-mail address. Let me know if you'd like me to inform you when a hotel accomplishes this.)

10. Tenacity

Growing a business is hard work. Customer acquisition and retention isn't an event. It isn't a new program. It is a way of thinking about customers. It is a way you go about business. It takes the right attitude, continual effort, and constant monitoring.

The question that should really matter in whether you are going to retain your customers and grow your business is not whether they are satisfied. The only question that matters is, "How likely are your customers to recommend you to their colleagues, their partners, their families, or to other people they do business with?"

If you're getting straight 10s on customer satisfaction, good for you. That means you're going to stay in business at least another year or two. That's nice, but not enough. If you get straight 10s on whether people would recommend your company to someone else, now you've really got something going on. You are not just going to survive. You are going to grow. At PrintingForLess.com, fully one-third of their new customers come from referrals. How does that compare with your business? Think about how much impact that has on the company's marketing budget, customer acquisition costs, or lifetime value of customers.

Sometimes a big business can show a dedication to tenacity from which we can all learn. Here's one from my experience. I drive a GS 300 Lexus. I'll admit that I bought my first one in

1993 because I thought it was pretty. It looked great and I could afford it, so I bought it.

I bought my second one last year because the first one was the best vehicle I've ever driven. It looked good, it was reliable, and it was extremely affordable. I would go so far as to say it was a bargain. Now that may sound strange when talking about a luxury car. Yes, the purchase price was high, but in terms of total cost of ownership, I would say it's sure to be a better deal than a Mercedes or BMW and probably even better than any car that is half its price.

I paid $32,000 for my first GS 300. It got good gas mileage. I never got stranded beside the road. Repair costs were next to nothing, especially in relation to other cars my family and I have owned. Quite simply, it was the best car I had ever owned. After driving it for eight years and 144,000 miles, I sold it for $10,000. What other highly reliable, fully loaded car can you think of that you can drive for so long for so little? From my perspective, the real Lexus selling point is a value proposition. The fact that it also has luxury appointments and performance is just icing on the cake.

But one small thing did go wrong. The cup holder, which was very important to me, my wife, and my son, broke twice. It broke, I got it fixed, it broke again, I got it fixed again, and then I sold the car.

This new GS 300 Lexus is superior in every way to my first one. It's faster, it gets better gas mileage, and it's more comfortable. The thing that really impressed me, however, was the cup holder. It is totally redesigned, in a way that makes more sense. I can't imagine how it could break. I am now not only satisfied but also thrilled enough to be telling everyone about this car. And what pushed me over the top was a part that probably costs less than $10.

But the people who designed this car did it right. They kept striving for improvement. They listened to their customers and watched their customers react to the car. The European automakers, at that time, turned their noses up at even putting cup holders in cars and concentrated on engineering and handling. ("Those stupid Americans—they shouldn't be drinking coffee in their car anyway. Don't they realize this is a work of art?") The American car companies cut corners wherever they could and continued to underperform on the price/value proposition they offered. Meanwhile, a Japanese car company personally showed me why they always come out on top with both critics and customers. One tiny thing went wrong with my old model, and they fixed it in the next model.

Think of how easy it would have been for this behemoth of a company to rest on their recent laurels. They're tenacious, and they refuse to be satisfied with just being the best. There has been no bigger success story in the automotive industry than Toyota, owner of the Lexus brand. When I bought my first Lexus, Toyota was the fifth-largest auto manufacturer in the world. Now they are the second largest.

Strive for continual improvement and refinement in the areas that customers care about most, even if those seem insignificant to you.

SUGGESTED NEXT STEPS

1. Look at your most recent invoices to see if your company is customer driven or internally focused.

2. Consider your training program. Be sure new hires are given a full indoctrination in who your unique customers are and why they buy from you instead of the other guys.

3. List all the ways in which you currently "touch" customers. Prioritize each based on how important it is to a customer. Set about improving the priorities.

4. Look for ways in which technology can improve your customer acquisition and retention. Implement your biggest "bang for the buck." (Hint: It will probably have something to do with e-mail.)

5. Look for your own version of the Milkshake Story (products and services your customers ask for that you could easily deliver but don't currently offer).

7

RULE 5:
PUT THE POWER
OF TECHNOLOGY
TO WORK

We shape our tools and then our tools shape us.

—Marshall McLuhan

I have a pretty good idea of what you think this chapter is going to be about. Chances are you're wrong, so read on. I begin with a little-known tale of technology to help illustrate what technology really means to you and me.

My family lives a good portion of the year in the Yucatan Peninsula area of Mexico, in a city called Mérida. Just 100 years ago, Mérida boasted of having the highest number of millionaires per capita of any city in the world. It was a boom-town like no other. The story of how those millionaires got there and how they lost it is an interesting tale.

For a couple thousand years, prior to the arrival of the Spanish, the Mayans controlled all of the Yucatan Peninsula and into what is now Guatemala, Belize, Honduras, and El

Salvador. The Mayans thought that the henequen plant was a gift from the gods because of all its various properties. The plant looks like the agave cactus—the same family that produces tequila. The Mayans used its fibers to make string, hammocks, rugs, and even clothing.

When the Spanish arrived, they were mostly interested in gold, glory, and God. Once the conquering was complete and they began to really settle the area, the ones who stuck around built haciendas (ranches) where they raised cattle and other livestock. Over the next 300 years, the Spanish empire went into steady decline. The French moved in during the mid-1800s and ended up building more haciendas and mansions. Even when Mexico took over the Yucatan and the country secured its independence, the European descendents stayed on and continued to run their enterprises.

As they started to see the potential of the henequen plant's fibers, the hacienda owners built production facilities to turn the fibers into rope, twine, and burlap sacks. They discovered ways to get this "sisal" rope and twine up to the cotton farmers in the United States, who were shipping their cotton out as fast as they could to the factories in the United States and Europe. The advantages of this product over the old wire baling previously used caused exploding demand. With the invention of the steam-powered shredding machine in the 1880s, the henequen industry really took off. Production kept expanding, to the point where 90 percent of the rope and burlap used in the world in the late 1800s came from this "green gold." World commercial shipping was also taking off at the time, which increased demand for large gauge ropes used to tether the ships in port. By 1900, the Yucatan was estimated to be the richest state in Mexico, and the economy was booming. Mansions were going up everywhere you looked. There were more than 650 haciendas in the area, and the nearby ports were bustling with traffic.

As with most near monopolies, it couldn't last, even though the hacienda owners probably thought their amazing income was permanent. First, other countries started growing their own plants and making cheaper henequen products. But the real blow came from synthetics, which were introduced in the 1930s and got steadily cheaper over the years, dealing a huge blow to natural fibers. The Yucatan growers saw a short spike during World War II, but by the 1950s, the industry was in steep decline. By the 1970s, most of the haciendas were all but abandoned. These days, production levels in the Yucatan have fallen to 12 percent of their peak output.

Most of the formerly grand haciendas are now in either total decay or have been restored by wealthy buyers or hotel developers. The ones that are still functioning as a production business are more of a novelty than a thriving company.

So what's the point of this obscure story about a low-tech product? The lesson here is that the business owners who ruled this market for more than 100 years defined themselves as cultivators and processors of sisal products. They were product driven, not customer driven. Instead of being focused on what solution they provided to shipping companies, they focused on a single plant and what you could make from it. Instead of having their eyes open to the potentially disruptive technologies targeting their industry, they continually focused on the status quo. Any of them could have seen what was coming and adapted. They could have been producing petroleum-based synthetics themselves with their cheap labor and shipping them out via their very close port. The Yucatan even has petroleum right off its shore. Or, they could have used their expertise to develop other products for the shipping industry. If they had, they might still be raking in the money today.

Let's contrast the Yucatan story with a U.S. rope company, Wall Industries. The company employs around 50 people and is based in North Carolina. I've gained permission to quote from the "company history" section of their web site (http://www.wallrope.com) because I think their story says it all:

Wall was incorporated in 1830 and has been held by the original family since its inception. Wall was founded by William Wall in Brooklyn, New York. The company expanded and moved to Beverly, NJ, in 1896. Over the years, the company continued to grow and expanded to six separate divisions. The Beverly rope manufacturing facility, encompassing 28 acres, was specifically designed to manufacture natural fiber rope. It became obsolete due to the development of synthetic fiber pioneered by the collective efforts of Wall, Dupont, and Philips Petroleum that replaced natural raw materials. Thereafter Wall focused entirely on the manufacture of synthetic rope and the need for the enormous Beverly facility with a deep water dock and railroad diminished. The decision to relocate to a modern facility in North Carolina was accomplished in 1981. Throughout Wall's history, it has survived the Civil War, the Spanish-American War, two World Wars, the Korean War, and the Vietnam conflict by being able to adapt to economic, technological, and market changes. Wall continues its rich history of state-of-art product development, diversification, and superior quality of products and service.

Wall Industries realized its business wasn't growing plants and making rope. Its business was providing a binding solution for shipping companies and other industries. The solution didn't change, just the materials and the means of delivery. By leveraging the latest and greatest technology, Wall not only survived but also thrived. By ignoring technological advancement, the Yucatan Peninsula became one of the poorest regions in North America (before Cancun came along).

Do you think technology can't do this to you? It can, but the difference is that it won't take 30 or 40 years; it might take only 3 or 4 years. For proof, you need only to look at how fast Polaroid slipped into bankruptcy or how Xerox and AT&T went from dominant giants to also-rans. Or, what about your local travel agent, music store, or TV repair shop?

WE GET USED TO WHAT'S HERE NOW

This story about the decline of henequen may feel like something that happened a million years ago, but it wasn't very long ago at all. My great-grandmother was alive during both the boom and the bust, and I knew her well.

The refrigerator seems like it has been around forever, but my mother still calls it an icebox. The first NASA engineers, many of them still working today, used slide rules to figure out how to put a man on the moon. There was a time, not so long ago, when I played vinyl albums on my hi-fi, played the new Pong video game for hours, and listened to progressive rock music featuring the newfangled Moog synthesizer. (My 13-year-old son still can't understand why I call a CD an "album.") In one defining moment in July of 1965, Bob Dylan "plugged in" at the Newport Jazz Festival and changed the sound of pop music forever. Amplified music that had heretofore been mostly the domain of teeny-boppers and blues enthusiasts suddenly became a popular creative force. By adopting technology, Dylan angered a significant portion of his "customer base," but opened up an enormous new market of baby boomers who were gravitating toward a more electric sound being popularized by the Beatles and the rest of the British Invasion.

What are you offering right now that will go the way of the sextant, the slide rule, or the acoustic "folky" singer? It's not too difficult to see these events coming if you keep your eyes open and recognize the signals. In 10 years, will we still see pay phones, film cameras, VCRs, or stock exchange trading floors? Will anything be made from "partially hydrogenated vegetable oil"? Many products hitting the shelf right now will be obsolete in the time it takes for one of our kids to make it through college. At the accelerated level we're moving now, product and service cycles in some industries will be measured in months, not years.

In the first half of the twentieth century, Harvard economist Joseph Schumpeter coined the famous phrase "creative destruction" to describe the ongoing process that is capitalism. When the waves of creative destruction are heading your way, you have two choices: either drown or learn to ride the waves.

WHAT IS TECHNOLOGY?

These days, when we hear the word *tech* or *technology,* we tend to think of computers, the Internet, software, and chip-driven electronic gadgetry. That aspect, however, is a very recent development in a long line of disruptive technologies. To me, technology encompasses a much broader range, such as physics, chemistry, biology, medicine, and agriculture.

According to NASA estimates, the universe is around 13.7 billion years old. Our little planet has been around only the past 4.5 billion of those years. The human race has been here in some form for a mere 2 to 2.5 million years, depending on whose estimate you like best, but *Homo sapiens* didn't appear until, at most, 150,000 years ago. So, in the history of the planet we call Earth, we *Homo sapiens* have been here only a tiny fraction of 1 percent of the time. We didn't invent agriculture until the end of the last Ice Age (around 13,000 years ago) but from that point on technology has been the driving force changing who we are as people.

Archeologists and anthropologists use our tools to define who we were and who we are as human beings. The Stone

Age, the Iron Age, the Bronze Age, and the Industrial Age all refer to our evolution as innovators of technology.

When we began to craft tools, people began to specialize. Some scholars even hypothesize that it was our early development of tools that led to a need for language. Our tool-making ability and the ability to disseminate information led to the building of civilizations. The world of industry and commerce could not have developed in the way that it has without continual innovation in our tools and our ability to communicate. In the book *Guns, Germs and Steel* (New York: Norton, 1999), Jared Diamond points out that the surface reason some societies took over the world while others became the conquered was mostly a matter of technology: "Technology, in the form of weapons and transport, provides the direct means by which certain peoples have expanded their realms and conquered other people." Diamond devotes most of his book to figuring out how people got to that point, but the end result was that technology created the competitive advantages, whether it was advanced agriculture, better ships, better swords, or guns.

Consider the impact that the following now-standard items had on sociology, history, and business. Before paper, we wrote on rags or papyrus. Before the steam engine, we didn't cross land or ocean without either the wind or animals to slowly get us there. Before the elevator, buildings could not go up more than a few stories. The Panama Canal digging failed the first time not because of engineering hurdles, but because we didn't have good enough medicine: Too many workers kept dying from diseases. When Abraham Lincoln was shot in 1865, the news had to literally cross the ocean by ship before Europe found out about it. By the time Krakatoa erupted in 1883, the incident quickly became a global news event due to the widespread use of the telegraph and undersea cables.

As difficult as it is to imagine now, many foundations of a typical office didn't exist in the twentieth century. It wasn't too long ago when nobody had a telephone, a typewriter, an electric light bulb, a car, or—for better or for worse—a coffee maker or vending machine. Even 20 years ago, when I began my career in advertising, the typical office operated far differently than it does today. (See the Not-So-Futuristic 1984.)

If you feel as though the current changes in technology are disruptive, consider the following list, developed over just a 20-year period, from 1780 to 1800:

- Bifocal lens
- Hot air balloon
- Power loom
- Threshing machine
- Steamboat
- Gas lighting
- Pencils
- Cotton gin
- Hydraulic press
- Lithography
- Smallpox vaccination
- Electric battery

What would you have done then—when you finally found out the news months or years later—if you were a cotton farmer, ink well maker, shipbuilder, or weaving factory owner? Would you fight change with all your might? Would you dismiss the newfangled inventions as a fad? Or would you figure out where these technologies could take you and grow faster than you ever imagined? Would you have had the ability to single out these innovations at an early stage? After all, around this same time, Ben Franklin was coming up with successful inventions such as the bifocal lens and the lightning rod. He also invented lightning bells, however, which were designed to ring whenever electricity was in the air. Unlike his more successful projects, these went over like a lead balloon.

Zoom ahead to the early years of a new century, and we find these changes equally dramatic but happening faster and faster. I'm not one of those "living on chaos" consultants who is going to tell you to continually throw everything you know out the window and reinvent yourself every week. Yes, technological changes create opportunities, and you need to be aware of them, but they are the tool, not the driver. Your sense of purpose can and should remain resolute. For example, just consider the motion picture industry. Between 1972 and 2002, this industry grew from a $1.4 billion industry to a $15 billion industry. Despite this incredible rate of growth, you would have lost your shirt had you bet on the wrong technological horse: drive-in movies, Betamax, or laser discs. Mindlessly jumping on the hottest new trend has been the downfall of countless companies. I've seen just as many companies fail, however, because they are late to recognize the transformative power of a compelling innovation.

Some technologies are passing fads. When a new development is going to cause an undeniable change in the marketplace, however, you need to move on it. This is what is commonly called a *disruptive technology,* and it is the real deal. The steam engine, the electric light bulb, the automobile, the airplane, and plastic are examples of developments that fundamentally changed entire industries. For that matter, so did more humble objects such as the fountain pen, the twin-blade razor, and the ball bearing.

INFORMATION TECHNOLOGY—
THEN AND NOW

Some of the most disruptive developments of all have involved information technology. In the past decade, the most dramatic disruptions have been caused by two factors: affordable and tiny computer technology and the World Wide Web. No matter how low-tech your business may be, those two items are either your nemesis or your opportunity. They are permanently altering the business landscape.

The Web is just a natural evolution, however, in a long line of disruptive information technology developments. The first true information technology began with Gutenberg's printing press, back in the mid-1400s. There are a lot of parallels between this introduction and what is happening today. This single technological development radically altered the course of history. You could argue that one German innovator's rudimentary contraption led to the Protestant Reformation, the migration to the "new world," and the spread of representative government.

I know 500 years seems like a long time ago, but in the context of human existence, it's as if it happened last week. We are still just on the cusp of developing the information technology that will shape our tools and drive our future. Let me say this in another way. In 20 years, the ways in which we use information technology now will seem as antiquated as the pony express.

Why should you care about what happened 500 years ago, or 100, or even 20? Because technology is the most important factor in our history. It has shaped us since the dawn of agriculture. The only thing that has changed is the rapid rate at which technology builds on itself and continues to expand at an exponential rate. I believe we are just getting started. Biotech is still in its toddler stage, and nanotech is

The Not-So-Futuristic 1984

Within two months of graduating from Miami University, I began my career working in advertising agencies. The year was 1984, and while we did not recognize it at the time, we were far from a technological utopia. As a bottom-rung junior account executive, I rarely got to participate in the sexy stuff commonly associated with the advertising biz. Sure, every once in a while I got to sit in on a focus group. Once a year, if I was a good boy, I got to help shoot a TV commercial. But the vast majority of my time was spent as a glorified proofreader—not a proofreader of creative media copy, but instead an editor of an endless stream of internal position papers and unnecessarily long client directives. Looking back on it now, I see that the technology we were using to produce these documents was hopelessly inefficient.

A photocopy of a hand-typed, 50-page report produced by my boss's boss would hit my desk on Monday morning. I would meticulously dissect this document, looking for everything from typos to fundamental factual errors. This process would take two days, including fact-checking time in our internal research library. Once I had written my changes and corrections in longhand, I would resubmit the document to the typing pool. They would make corrections to the document with old-fashioned correction tape, or later, the newfangled innovation known as white-out fluid. If they weren't too busy pounding out more important reports on their IBM Selectrics, I might be able to get the corrected document back within 24 hours. I would then forward my work up the chain of command, where inevitably additional changes would be made and insertions would be added. It was not unusual for a document like this to reappear on my desk three or four times over the course of the next two weeks, each requiring a new bottle of white-out and a sapling's worth of internal photocopies.

(Continued)

(Continued)

Once we had gotten it to the point of internal approval, we would then send a fax of the document to the client (because everyone was in a hurry for this information). At that time, the fax machine was about the size of a car and required a trained operator. I would stand in line to get my document faxed, along with all of the other lowly junior account executives. Sometimes a box of chocolates or a ticket to the baseball game was required to get my work to the front of the line. It would take nearly two hours to get a 50-page document faxed.

The document would then go through a similar process of checks and balances within the halls of the client. With any luck, our report could be finalized and approved by the uppity ups in less than a month.

I don't work in an advertising agency today, but I've talked with some who do. For these young people, this office nightmare seems almost unbelievable. Word processing is ubiquitous, and 5-year-olds understand the cut and paste function. Spell-check now even cleans up sentence fragments and poor grammar. Portions of documents can be freely, easily, and quickly disseminated throughout the organization, allowing for broader collaboration. The World Wide Web now makes fact checking a breeze. Getting out a 50-page report to a client today can certainly be accomplished in a day or two with the same level of accuracy and insightfulness.

But here's the "so what?" I am certain that as incredible as this paper maze contrast may seem, it will be nothing in comparison to where we'll be in 2024. Yes, we have come a long way in terms of office efficiency, but clearly we have much further to go.

Every year, around the time of the Super Bowl, TV programs rerun a now-famous Apple Macintosh ad that aired only once in 1984. At the time, it had a profound impact on how we viewed the future of technology. Yes, we've come a long way since then, but we haven't seen anything yet.

just a newborn. Unavoidable waves of technological change are headed for your company and your industry, no matter what industry you are in. You need to recognize and prepare for them.

THE WORLD WIDE WEB: ONE EXAMPLE OF CREATIVE DESTRUCTION

The first time I logged on to the World Wide Web, way back in 1994, it blew my mind. I knew that this would radically change the business landscape. My first thought was, "There go the travel agents." To me, it was plain as could be that their days were numbered. The only question was how fast it was going to happen. Here we are, 10 years later, and the corner travel agent has gone the way of the milkman. The ones that have survived have found a new focus: either peddling high-margin cruises and package deals or catering to the high-end adventure traveler who has far more money than time. They can't make a profit any other way.

The same thing has happened to many other professionals who relied on exclusive access to information. Stockbrokers, real estate agents, and doctors, for instance, have all lost some of their leverage.

In 1996, I was asked to present information about this thing called the Internet and the World Wide Web to insurance executives in various companies in Hartford, Connecticut. While there were a few IT people interested in what I was saying, the real decision makers just heard science fiction. It was like they were patting me on the head and saying, "Kid, you just don't understand our business. This isn't going to work for our industry." You can probably guess what happened. For some, it did work. Soon, the slow movers got gobbled up by more forward-thinking rivals. Others are struggling and will never catch up with the companies who saw the potential.

They couldn't get past how they would fit the current way they did things into that model. Some could understand how it might make for a better brochure, but the transactional aspect of the Web was seen as, "not in my lifetime."

WE'VE SURPASSED THE MOST FROTHY ESTIMATES

By 1998, amid the fever-pitch hoopla of the Internet madness, some enthusiastic people made crazy estimates about how fast the World Wide Web would be adopted. They created charts showing rapidly accelerating growth in Internet use in homes, transaction growth over the Internet, broadband rollout, and so on. Even the cheerleaders were a bit hesitant to endorse the numbers. Critics sneered: "You're telling me Americans will spend $10 billion over their computers, using their credit cards? You've got to be joking!"

Guess what happened? We've blown right past those numbers and left most of them in the dust. In December 2003 alone, consumers spent $18.5 billion shopping online. By 2007, Jupiter Research expects business-to-consumer e-commerce sales to be $133 billion. On the business-to-business side, yearly transaction numbers are in the trillions. Getting a handle on how many trillions is getting more and more difficult—some international businesses are doing 100 percent of their buying and selling over the Web.

Forget the dot-com meltdown. Forget the tales of spectacular crashes and deflated bubbles. Reality is that the Internet has only grown and become more important during the past few years. Let's look at the post-bubble market capitalization of a few marquee names. The *market capitalization* is the share price times the number of shares outstanding; in essence, it is the value the shareholding public has put on the company.

As I wrote this chapter, eBay had a market capitalization of nearly $50 billion. To put that in perspective, it was higher than Boeing, Gillette, or Disney and double that of General Motors. (Keep in mind that eBay did not even exist until 1995.) If eBay were a country, in 2004 it would have been about the 55th wealthiest in the world, worth more than Morocco, Vietnam, or Kuwait. Despite this size, the company's revenues grew nearly 80 percent that fiscal year and is expected by most analysts to grow at least 30 percent per year for the foreseeable future. Profit margins are huge, and the company throws off a tremendous amount of cold, hard cash.

Amazon has defied all its critics and kept on growing. The company's market cap often floats up to $20 billion, and in 2004 the company was worth twice as much as Sears. Amazon was expected to book close to $7 billion in revenue that year. It is still growing at a clip of 30 to 40 percent per year. Not bad for a virtual company with a very small hard asset base.

One of the most visible casualties of the dot-com meltdown was online pet retailers. Don't tell that to PetMed Express. It was ranked as the top hot-growth company out of 100 high flyers in a 2004 *BusinessWeek* article (Special Report, "Hot Growth Companies," June 7, 2004). It sells pet prescriptions direct to consumers by various methods, but over half its business comes through the Internet. Its approximately 150 employees generate over $30 million per quarter in revenue. Sales and profits both grew over 100 percent in the past year.

The business-to-business cases might not be as well known but are equally impressive.

Oracle sells and supports database software. That's pretty much all the company does. They generated over $10 billion in revenue in 2003—a terrible year for tech companies—and $2.6 billion of that was net profit. That's some serious money. In terms of market cap, their worth hovered around $55 billion in late 2004. Oracle software is a tool, so let's compare that to some traditional toolmakers. To equal the market worth of Oracle when I wrote this, you would have needed to add *all* of the following tool makers together: Caterpillar, Black & Decker, American Standard, Whirlpool, Maytag, Stanley Works, Snap-on, and Electrolux. And that's just Oracle. There are other technology companies that are even bigger.

Symantec makes the Norton line of computer security products. In essence, they insure your computer against illness in the form of viruses. In 2004, the market valued them at around $14 billion. Let's compare that value to companies who insure the health of us human beings. Many of those are private, but to give you an idea of how Symantec is valued, the company is worth more than Cigna or Aetna.

I know you may be looking at this and thinking it's all about big companies and that it doesn't apply to you. Please don't fool yourself. These same incredible shifts in competitive advantage and value creation are happening in your backyard right now.

MACRO IS THE STORY

I probably don't know much about your business. I certainly don't know as much about it as you do. I can't tell you what kind of technology matters for your business. Maybe it's the hottest new imaging software, the latest electron microscope, or just a better kind of nail gun. There are probably a dozen tech-related initiatives out there that could improve your business and help you make more profit, but you need to be the one to know what those are, based on your sense of purpose and your goals. If you hire the right people and keep yourself well informed, you'll figure out what those are. (See the 50-Mag Solution in Chapter 4.)

Most growing private companies embrace technological change. Academic and consultant studies have backed this up, finding that the positive attitude toward technology is one of the key factors determining the likelihood of growth.

Growing companies are more likely to use technology-driven solutions to achieve a superior position. They also emphasize the adoption of technology internally to create better efficiencies, serve customers better, and launch innovative products and services faster.

However, what really matters to any growing business is the macrostory. What is the big picture? How can technology help you do what you are currently doing even better—cheaper, faster, more efficiently, or more impressively to your customers? How can technology open up new product/service lines or new markets? How can technology help you become a high-growth business? Conversely, what threats will you face in the future if you adopt a wait-and-see attitude toward emerging technology? What is coming down the pike that is going to transform how you operate?

YOU ARE IN TECH WHETHER YOU LIKE IT OR NOT

We have reached a point where no matter what business you are in, you are knee-deep in technology. Farmers, steel makers, ice cream store owners, and landscapers are not exempt—the standouts in these supposedly low-tech businesses are often using technology to blow away their competitors.

Many would argue that Wal-Mart's dominance started long before they got so huge; they've had an operational edge for more than two decades because their supply chain technology was better. General Electric's management and planning philosophy get a lot of press, but what you don't read so often is how much of the company's business has moved to the Internet—billions and billions of it every month.

You don't need to be one of the biggest corporations in the world to make the most of technology. In just the past few years, I've witnessed a tremendous number of seemingly "old world" companies that have been transformed by the latest technology. The Candlewic Company of Doylestown, Pennsylvania, has grown their candle- and soap-making supplies business by leaps and bounds over the past few years. Technology has allowed owners Bill and Dave Binder to reach and serve a much broader market of resellers and enthusiasts. From the point of automated order entry all the way through the UPS-designed "pick and pack" system, technology now allows Candlewic to deliver on what their customers really want: small, infrequent purchases. These orders would have been wholly unprofitable just a few short years ago. Now this segment encompasses most of their growth.

In 1995, a company called Tool Shack was a small, one-location commercial tool reseller in Las Vegas, Nevada. Today, Mytoolstore.com, run by the same team, has grown into a multimillion dollar online trailblazer. While most small tool resellers are shaking in their work boots over big-box retailers such as Home Depot and Lowe's, MyToolStore.com ships well-known brands such as Makita, Bosch, and Ingersoll-Rand to all 50 states and 90 countries around the world. Who would have guessed that technology would allow a Nevada-based company to grow with sales into Asia, Latin America, and the Caribbean? Sprint named the company "2002 Innovative Business of the Year" because of its outstanding application of technology to grow and enhance the business.

Remember PrintingForLess.com? Here's another company in an old world industry that, every day, is doing things that couldn't have been done a few years ago. From their sophisticated customer acquisition modeling, to their proprietary press utilization software, technology is at the very core of how this company continually redefines what it means to be a commercial printer.

Candles, tools, and printing—none of these products are new. However, the way in which these companies meet and

A Finger on the Pulse—From Anywhere

Digital cable television continues to grow throughout this country. Some industry pundits believe that our cable companies will soon be bringing us everything from telephone service to point-to-point video conferencing. Right now, for most of us, digital cable means a better image and on-demand movies.

It will probably come as no surprise for you to know that the cable television industry has suffered for years from a reputation for lousy service, especially on the phone. And they know it. If they are going to provide all of these other services in the future, they have to meet your need on your existing services. That's where iGLASS Networks comes in.

Founders Tim Bolden, George Woodring, and Jack Woodring have designed at least a partial solution for cable operators. Let's say you and the family order the latest Jim Carrey movie on screen, using your digital remote. Despite having clicked all the right buttons and responding properly to the subsequent prompts, the movie isn't playing. The natives are restless; something has to be done. If this problem had occurred before iGLASS came along, you probably would have experienced some frustration. If you've ever been caught up in the labyrinths of on-hold, phone tree loops and ineffectual suggestions, you know what I'm talking about. iGLASS Networks' solution takes the pain away for both cable operators and their customers—you and me. Their remote software product monitors network operation center (NOC) for any and all glitches, outages, and other problems.

At the first sign of trouble, the monitoring software automatically kicks out a notice to NOC personnel. Each member of the iGLASS team has a wireless Handspring Treo 600 device. Through Internet protocol (IP) technology, the on-duty iGLASS

(Continued)

(Continued)

employee receives an easy-to-interpret warning. The employee can see which node is giving the problem, suggestions on how it might be solved, and a list of phone numbers to contact to discuss these potential solutions. In many cases, the operator taking your disgruntled service call can truthfully let you know the problem has been identified, addressed, and solved.

In a recent conversation I had with founder and president Tim Bolden, he described for me what technology has meant for his company:

> Technology has been an enabler for us. Without it, a company our size could never attempt what we have accomplished.
>
> Ten years ago, we would not have been able to build iGLASS. The cost of the communication lines alone would have been prohibitive to a company our size. Now with low-cost cable modems and virtual private network devices, we can build a nationwide network very inexpensively. Current communication technology allows us and our customers to use our tools from practically anywhere. I can access our system in my pajamas at home.
>
> Network operation centers have traditionally been the domain of large corporations with lots of money, lots of equipment, and lots of people. We have been able to use technology to accomplish the same thing with a minimal investment, limited equipment, and only a few people.

I love this story. It clearly shows what is really happening out there with technology. A product that has been with us for only a few years (digital cable) has quickly reached a point where service levels have become an issue. The really smart guys at iGLASS saw the emerging need before any others and set about building a solution. Folks, I've seen the solution and while I'm no cutting-edge engineer, I honestly believe I could work in a service role for the company. The easy-to-see, simple-to-understand interface makes most problem resolution a snap. That's what technology offers: not more complications but, instead, more elegant solutions.

exceed customer expectations is truly new. I also know companies that literally could not have existed until recently. I have worked with a company called iGLASS Networks. This seven-employee firm has managed to take a previously complicated problem and, through technology, find a simpler, more elegant solution. (See A Finger on the Pulse—From Anywhere.)

Consider what the following Inc. 500 companies were able to do first:

- CourtSmart Digital Systems installs systems in courtrooms that allow lawyers and judges to leave the courtroom carrying a DVD of the day's proceedings. They also created a digital system to allow police to record interrogations and polygraphs. With 18 employees, the company generated $4.4 million in revenue in its last reported calendar year.
- Microtek uses technology to set up a complete outsourced training center for companies, handling registrations, printing of manuals, and other logistics through a web interface. With 60 employees, the company generated $14.5 million in its last fiscal year.
- CityXpress is a Canadian company that has its main sales office in Seattle. Using technology that didn't exist a few years ago, it sets up joint auctions between 200 newspapers and local business owners. The owners get advertising credit for selling extra inventory, the papers get a cut, and CityXpress gets paid a fee. Through technology, everybody wins. The company went from 12 to 45 employees in two years, with several hundred percentage points in revenue and profit growth.

I'm not going to go into all the ways technology can help you save money and do your job better. Frankly, you can only do that yourself. However, I do want to point out that you no longer have a financial excuse for not using information technology to your advantage. Off the shelf, for a few hundred dollars or less, you can buy top-tier software programs to manage your accounting, web page design, documents, and other day-to-day tasks. You can subscribe to online services that do a great job of salesforce management, supply chain management, auctioning of unsold inventory, payroll, targeted mailings, or most any other function the big guys are doing. You can buy a box the size of a briefcase that uses sophisticated voice recognition to route your phone calls—even sending them to a designated cell phone.

Technology allows you to innovate. There are literally thousands of private enterprises out there using technology to create businesses that couldn't have existed a few years ago. I'm no psychic, but I can promise you the same thing will be happening a decade from now, only faster. Fast-growing companies are now offering customized services or products. They're drilling down into data to find the perfect customer fits for their tiny niche. They're creating new partnerships to meet customer demands. In short, they're using new technology to do what they have always done even better. Perhaps most importantly, leading companies are sending the right message to the right prospects at the right time. Technology enables growth.

The key is figuring out what your real business is and then riding those waves of creative destruction wherever they lead. Figure out what your solution is—not what your product or service is. Then offer that solution, whatever the means of delivery turns out to be.

BECOME AN EXPERT, OR HIRE ONE RIGHT NOW

To take advantage of all this, however, you need to be an expert. You need to know what's out there, what works, and what can help your business. You need to know what is on the way and how it is going to create obstacles or opportunities in the future. No matter what business you are in, you have to become a technology expert.

The best way I know to become an expert is to fully immerse yourself in technology as it relates to your business and industry. Really talk to the technology vendors at the next trade show—not just the salespeople but also the behind-the-scenes product developers who build the solutions or applications. Find out who writes the technology columns in your trade publications and become their friend. Offer them valuable insights into how your business is looking at technology, and then, perhaps, they can offer a unique perspective on other areas that might warrant your attention. Journalists like this are dying for someone like you to call. You can even invite a professor from the local community college to use your company as a case study for a business, computer science, or engineering class.

If you truly can't get your hands around it and understand it, hire someone who can be that expert and can explain it to you regularly in terms that make sense. Your company needs to be on top of the tech trends that are shaping your industry. In Chapter 4, when talking about superior market intelligence, one of the things you are going to be looking for is disruptive technologies affecting other industries, geographies, and even individuals.

This doesn't mean you adopt every new gadget that comes along or that you are always on the bleeding edge of what's being pushed into the marketplace. Plenty of companies spent millions on things such as fancy CRM software, only to find they didn't have the internal processes or people in place to really use it. Or even worse, they didn't have the internal expertise to interpret the data the software produces. The money

Who Won? Who Lost?

The history books love to talk about winners and losers. Let's look at the ripple effect some past disruptive technologies created.

THE AUTOMOBILE

As the automobile reached critical mass, it literally transformed America. It led to highways, suburbs, travel destinations, shopping malls, and a general spreading out of cities and towns.

- Who won? Homebuilders, road builders, steel makers, rubber companies, the lawn care industry, oil refiners, tourist attractions, big box retailers, convenience stores, and states such as Florida and California.
- Who lost? Trolley car makers, railroads, corner grocery stores, downtown department stores and movie theaters, milk and potato chip deliverymen, and much of the Northeast and Midwest.

REFRIGERATION

When commercial and then consumer refrigeration technology came along, the whole food industry was transformed.

- Who won? Industrial food processors, fishermen, fruit importers, packaging companies, and appliance makers.
- Who lost? Local farmers, retail butchers, ice delivery companies, icebox makers, and anyone else who lost their share of the local stomach.

THE WORLD WIDE WEB

In just 10 years, the Web went from a novelty to something that pervades our lives. Its impact hits a wide swath: research, shopping, supply chains, marketing, customer relations, financial

(Continued)

management, communication, media, entertainment, and many more.

- Who won? Anyone who saw the potential, but the big winner so far has been the consumer.
- Who lost? Old-guard middlemen, anyone who reacted too slowly, and anyone whose business was based on sole access to information: travel agents, insurance agents, car dealers, newspapers (especially classified ads), and encyclopedia publishers.

You could run this little exercise in your head for a long list of developments. Imagine what happened when steel, fuel oil, electricity, plastic, or air conditioning came along. For the business you are in, look for what could rock your cozy world and be ready to adapt.

would have been better spent on hiring the right people and training them well. By being an expert, however, or having a talented one at your disposal, you will know what your business can take advantage of and what is just a distraction.

SEE THE SIGNS

In the new millennium, your future depends on your recognition of disruptive technologies. You're not going to have 10 or 20 years to change course. You might have 2 years, 10 months, or 20 days. Information circles the globe in a nanosecond, so competitive innovations of any kind will enjoy a shorter and shorter time frame.

As I mentioned before, the Web has been in our lives for only 10 years or less, depending on when we each first logged on. Look at how radically some industries have been transformed during that time. I mentioned a few industries before, but here

Low-Tech Innovation

Henry Ford, Thomas Edison, Steven Jobs: All of these names are synonymous with the advancement of modern technology. But technology alone never would have made these people successful. It was their uncanny knack for innovation that really led to their unprecedented success and icon status. Ben Franklin famously harnessed the power of electricity, but it took more than a century before anyone found an innovative way to make a buck from it. I submit to you that these American icons should be remembered as innovators, not technologists. When evaluating any technology, the prudent growth-oriented small business owner should have marketable innovation as his or her goal.

To me, no one better personifies innovation than a Chicago baker named Jimmy Dewar. In the fall of 1930, Dewar noticed that the stack of shortcake pans resting in a corner of his bakery was used only a couple of months a year. But on that day, Dewar didn't see just a stack of pans. He saw an opportunity.

Dewar mixed together a pan full of sponge cake and sent it through the oven. He mixed up some crème and stuffed the cake with a core of the fresh filling. On a fall day in 1930, Jimmy Dewar took a pile of idle assets and created an American icon.

If you don't think that's innovative, ask one of the people who ate one of the half billion Twinkies produced last year.

To start thinking like a Jimmy Dewar, ask yourself the following questions:

- What are my current assets?
- How can I use them in new and better ways?
- Is there anywhere my existing assets can streamline my existing processes?
- Is there a new technology that might allow me to leverage my existing assets?

(Continued)

Jimmy Dewar innovated with technology available to most any other baker at that time. There was nothing special about his particular oven or his brand of pastry gun. It was a new way of looking at his existing technology that led to this revolutionary new product.

When considering your existing assets, leave no stone un-turned because nothing is too sacred, too special, or too perfect that it can't be improved on—even the Twinkie.

Just ask Chris Sell, a Brooklyn, New York, restaurateur who a few years back decided to batter-coat one of Dewar's creations and deep fry it. His result: hour-long lines of people wanting to pay $3 a pop for a deep-fried Twinkie. Terrible for our arteries, perhaps, but a great innovation for Mr. Sell.

So keep your eyes open. With a little ingenuity, innovation can be a piece of cake.

are more: book publishing, consumer retail, employment advertising, software, direct marketing, dating services, advertising, the recorded music industry, movie rentals, and package delivery. Within companies, the Web is influencing inventory control, shipping practices, employment screening, financial reporting, and a dozen other factors.

Most observers, even in the small business world, have been predicting this for years. A study titled *The Future of Small Business*, authored in 1999 by Dr. Richard W. Oliver, had the following quote in the executive summary:

While new opportunities created by technology seem limitless, some small firms, particularly those resistant to innovation, are threatened by these changes. The rapid pace of change associated with computerization and the Internet will force smaller firms to change even more effectively in the next 10 to 15 years. Adaptability, willingness to change, and the ability to execute are the mantra for the Internet era.

Looking back now, it seems unbelievable that anyone running a business didn't see this coming. It was like a big, fat, hairy monster stomping through Main Street, U.S.A., crushing buildings in its wake, shouting, "Look at me! Look at me!" Watch for the signs, so you're not the guy taking a nap on a park bench, about to be stomped on, who says, "What monster?"

At the beginning of this chapter, I tried to discourage any preconceived notions of what this technology chapter was going to be about. I hope that I provided you with at least a slightly new and broader perspective on a topic that has been discussed ad nauseam in the past few years. Much of this has more or less been said before, perhaps more directly by some and even more eloquently by others. My goal was to plainly outline a macroview of what technology means for you, in my humble opinion, from one small businessperson to another.

My big point is this: The role of technology in the human condition cannot be overstated. It has been with us since the dawn of civilization, and it will be even more pervasive in our near future. Don't allow the endless cycle of hype and disillusionment, boom and bust, and trial and error dissuade you from fully immersing yourself in technology for the growth of your business, growth of your employees, service of your customers, and, ultimately, growth of you as an innovative leader.

If you take one thing away from this chapter, it is this: Watch for the coming waves of technological innovation, and learn how to ride them. Over the next 10 years, regardless of your chosen field of endeavor, technological advancements will be more pervasive and impactful than ever before. Learn how to evaluate and implement these opportunities quickly, and assume that these tools are only temporary.

SUGGESTED NEXT STEPS

1. Review the opening henequen story. Determine how this lesson pertains to your business. Be sure to use the words *status quo* and *changing technology.*

2. Invite a number of hardware, software, and telecom firms to visit your business, and ask them to propose a way to save you money. In particular, ask them to look for mundane tasks that should be automated but currently are not.

3. Identify one or more experts who can assist you in your technology education.

4. Become the expert on how wireless technology will impact a business like yours.

5. Look at your existing tools and technology (not just information technology). Consider innovating in those areas in which your existing technology is underutilized.

8

RULE 6:

ATTRACT AND KEEP THE BEST AND THE BRIGHTEST

You're only as good as the people you hire.

—Ray Kroc

Since I have become a business growth expert, one question always comes up in media interviews: "What is the number one issue facing small business today?" When I first declared myself a growth expert, my answer was simply "money." It was accurate because that was small business's perception in the go-go days of the mid-1990s. The economy was really beginning to boom, opportunities abounded, and small business owners felt that the number one barrier to growth was access to capital to fuel expansion.

Now we are all a little wiser. Like most small business owners today, I now realize that the number one issue facing small business owners is the same today as it was since the first time an ancient craftsman hired an apprentice. It's all about the people—always has been, always will be.

I have traveled all around the country speaking with business owners like you. I have listened to your concerns about barriers to growth. Clearly, you, too, now understand that finding and retaining the very best and the very brightest is paramount.

In the most recent national election, it is interesting that politicians from both major parties were espousing their plans to generate more jobs. Newspapers and magazines kept referring to the economy as being in a "jobless recovery." Everyone kept talking about the lack of jobs.

But here's the funny thing. Small business owners have been telling me for years they can't find enough good people. This has always been especially true of growth companies. And it makes sense. It's difficult to see during recessions, but a shortage of skilled and semiskilled workers has been a fact of life in the U.S. economy for quite a while now.

This shortage affects many levels. I know of one business owner who has been unable to fill a $28,000 per year receptionist position for months now. With signs of an improving economy, business owners keep calling me with questions like, "Do you know where I can find a good vice president of . . . ?" Requests for senior sales, marketing, operations, and IT people seem to be the most common. Everyone knows that there is also a shortage in nurses, computer analysts, and network administrators. But who would have guessed that the factory floor is experiencing the same challenges? An August 2004 *Wall Street Journal* article even pointed to the growing need for qualified people to fill old economy jobs such as welders and machinists. In a National Association of Manufacturers' survey, 80 percent of responding businesses said they had a "moderate to serious" shortage of qualified job candidates.

The Bureau of Labor Statistics projects that between 2002 and 2012, there will be a need for 21.3 million new workers. They further predict only 17.4 million new workers will enter the labor market in that same period. Given this gap of nearly five million, there's a good reason you're finding it difficult to hire good people.

I wish I could tell you that this is a temporary situation, but it's not. A number of different studies that I've looked at come to the same conclusion. While factors ranging from the national economic rate of growth to future immigration laws will affect future employment trends, it appears likely that our greatest gap will come in the highest skill categories—those requiring a four-year college degree.

PAINFULLY OBVIOUS

Nothing is more important to the growth of any organization than finding, training, and retaining superior people. This is probably no big revelation to you. More than any of the rules I've discussed in this book, this concept is the most obvious. It is also the most irrefutable. However, everyone also knows that a proper diet and regular exercise is the key to a long and healthy life. Somehow, not enough of us take that irrefutable knowledge and put it into action. Instead, we look for the shortcuts and quick fixes: temporary programs with even more temporary results.

So, let me take this opportunity to make the following statement in the most emphatic way possible: Your job is people—period. End of story. I don't care if you fancy yourself a marketing expert, a technology expert, or a financial expert. If you plan to lead an organization that's trying to get to the next level, at some point, you become less involved in doing and more involved in leading. As I look back over my three experiences running fast-growth companies, it is now more apparent to me that I should have spent even more time on people than I did. And I spent more time on people than any of my contemporaries.

I did get one thing right, however. I hired expertise before the growth, not in reaction to it. This point is key. Most business owners put the cart before the horse. Don't wait for growth before you hire the best and brightest. You hire the best and brightest to enable you to grow.

A small business owner needs to continually find the best and brightest people available to achieve sustainable growth. People directly impact every other growth initiative.

So far in this book, I've talked about five rules that effect growth. Those five rules represent areas in which successful growth companies concentrate their efforts. Any initiatives in those areas will crash and burn, however, if you don't have good people who can make them happen. There is a direct correlation between retaining good people and retaining good customers. You can't build an effective growth plan without problem-solving minds. The best strategy in the world won't succeed if you don't have a highly skilled team that is capable of executing it.

WHERE DO WINNERS WANT TO WORK?

As discussed in Chapter 3, creating the right culture is your first step toward growth. A positive culture can become your magnet for attracting good people. Before you do anything, you need to create a company where top performers want to work. If you don't, you will never make it. You might fool a few superstars, but you'll have difficulty holding on to them for any length of time. This is true whether the unemployment rate in your area is 2 percent or 20 percent.

Your best employees also want to grow and learn. What are you doing to help them in this effort? Do you offer regular skills training? Do you help cover the cost of classroom courses or seminars? Do you send key people to trade shows or association conferences? Do you have an in-house resource library filled with materials for continuing education? Help your people improve, and they will help your company improve.

There are a number of surveys and books ranking the best companies to work for, and a number of business magazines have their own version. While the details may vary from survey to survey, some traits are common in almost all companies that top these lists:

- A sense of purpose that employees can believe in and relate to
- Extremely good two-way communication systems
- An emphasis on making people feel appreciated
- Rewards and recognition for superior performance and meeting goals
- Regular and meaningful training
- Flexible scheduling and vacation time
- An opportunity to advance

Note that "high salaries," "regular raises," and "end-of-year bonuses" do not figure in as prominently in these surveys as you might think. Money is important, but it is not the most important thing. You've probably seen the triangle often referred to as *Maslow's hierarchy*. Money is critical to meet our most fundamental needs, such as food, clothing, and shelter. Once you get past that level, it is only human nature to be searching for a more meaningful existence. We've all seen it time and time again—money can't buy happiness. Perhaps Maslow's insight into human motivation helps us understand why the higher you climb the salary ladder, the less important money becomes as a motivator. Think of a new hire's salary as poker stakes. You "ante up" to meet a person's basic needs. But what keeps your hand flush with the best and brightest takes a lot more than just an adequate paycheck.

Don't get me wrong: Money *is* a great way for people to keep score. For the employee and his or her family, money is an important yardstick for measuring a person's skills and accomplishments. But money in and of itself cannot, over a sustained period, build the level of dedication you need from every member of your organization. If people are going to devote most of their waking hours to your company, they want to feel that all that effort is going to accomplish something. They also want to feel they are getting something out of the deal besides a steady paycheck, especially if the company is meeting or exceeding its goals. The qualitative benefits become far more important over time than the numbers on a paycheck.

The great thing for you, as a private business owner, is that you can implement many of the things that employees care about without laying out a lot more cash. Unlike a big business, you can also do it without much bureaucracy. Public recognition costs very little. Aligning employees' goals with your own is just a matter of time and communication. Letting people work on a flexible schedule costs you nothing and can easily improve productivity.

Bonuses and awards will cost you something, but if you have set up the goals properly, even dramatic cash bonuses will have paid for themselves anyway. If a sales organization gets a 20 percent bonus for increasing sales by 50 percent, you should be jumping with joy when you write out those checks. If customer service people get a bonus each time a customer

writes a testimonial letter, you should look forward to handing out a hundred bonuses with a big smile on your face. Reward people for stretching, and you'll be amazed at what they
can do for your growth.

Don't assume, however, that bonuses have to involve a lot of
cash. I once had a 65-year-old sewing machine operator tell
me, with tears in her eyes, that no one had ever made her feel
as special as she did that day. Her bonus? A steak lunch with
her manager and me at the local Golden Corral. It never
ceases to amaze me how hard a group of inside sales reps will
work for one pizza party. Many people would rise to an occasion for an extra day of vacation.

When it comes to recognition and rewards, you have to get
creative. At Honest Tea, president Seth Goldman has developed a unique program that recognizes achievement and fos-
ters loyalty. Total cost for the program is zilch. Here's how it
works. Each Honest Tea product has a 10-digit UPC bar code
associated with it. The first five digits refer to the company itself. The second five digits are used to discern among their
various brands and flavors. Most companies put their products in a linear, sequential order. In other words, if the most
recent product's last five digits were 32027, the next product
to be developed would be 32028.

However, for an innovative company like Honest Tea, non-
linear thinking created an opportunity to motivate and
recognize employees. When somebody does something truly
outstanding at Honest Tea, the company allows that person to
pick the next UPC code. These outstanding employees use
their anniversary dates, birth dates, or lucky numbers. Whenever a new product is unveiled internally, the person who rose
above and beyond the call of duty is also recognized. It may
sound like a small gesture, but Goldman assures me the practice has had a serious impact on his ability to build loyalty

among his employees. "Giving people a sense of ownership is critical," says Goldman. "Sure, we've also done some equity sharing over the years, and that is very helpful, too. But in terms of immediacy, I'm not sure this UPC thing isn't just as effective."

A few years ago, a sales manager at Honest Tea lost his father, to whom he was very close. At the same time he was dealing with this tragic loss, the employee was also fully immersed in a particularly complicated negotiation process with a well-known, big-box retailer. Despite the potential for distraction, this manager hooked the big fish. Subsequently, and unbeknownst to the manager, the entire Honest Tea team decided to dedicate their latest product to the memory of the sales manager's father. "When we announced the newest code would be for this guy's father's birth date," says Goldman, "there were more than a few tears wiped away."

Try looking at creative options that are easy for you to implement. Can you give high achievers something useful from your company's inventory? Or, do you have a couple of seats for the local AAA baseball team? A prime parking space they can use for the quarter? Some product you can acquire though a barter arrangement with a partner? The reward has to be meaningful, but it doesn't have to cost a fortune. Always throw in lunch with the company president as well. It makes your guests feel special, and you just might hear the best idea of the year.

One last note: Be sure your recognition and rewards programs directly tie back to performance. Too often, I see antiquated, complicated "bonus" programs that employees simply don't understand. When it becomes difficult to correlate performance and reward, it becomes impossible to use the system as a motivator. I've seen employees who view their periodic bonuses as random acts of fate over which they have no real influence. The lesson seems to be "keep your head down and your hopes high."

YOU'RE NOT AT A DISADVANTAGE

Many small business owners take a defeatist attitude to hiring from the start, believing they could never compete with the IBM office across town or the Toyota factory in the next city over. True, these are world-class companies, so if you are comparing only things such as benefit packages or pay levels, it can indeed be difficult to compete. However, a look at most of those big company employees shows that there are weaknesses you can and should exploit.

According to a Gallup poll released in 2004, 61 percent of U.S. workers say they received no meaningful rewards or recognition for their efforts the previous year. (Wow!) An amazing 71 percent of workers consider themselves "disengaged"—clock-watchers who can't wait to go home.

If you still think you don't have the means to lure people away from big companies, here are a few statistics to chew on. These are what I call the *two-thirds axiom of the big business workforce.* Roughly two-thirds of big biz workers say:

- They have "just some" or "not much" trust that their employers will treat them fairly (Peter D. Hart Research Associates).
- Finding a better job would improve their quality of life (CareerBuilder).
- They would switch sectors/industries for the right opportunity (Robert Walters).
- Their boss has "no clue" of what to do to be a good manager (Delta Road).
- They would work for two-thirds of their current salary if they could move to a rural community that offered a

higher quality of life and a shorter commute time. (I must admit that this one is my highly unscientific polling of fellow travelers who have been stuck on an airplane with me over the years.)

Big businesses are, by definition, bureaucracies. Bureaucracies, by definition, become increasingly inefficient, inflexible, and slow to change. Big businesses are also notorious for narrowly defining a person's role in that company. Pigeonholing doesn't meet the need for new experiences and new learning that the best and brightest crave.

So think about it. You have an opportunity to entice today's most desirable workers. But you need to understand their ever-changing needs and motivations.

People want:

- Meaning
- Purpose
- Understanding
- Family
- Health
- Self-expression
- Less "working"
- More "living"

Therefore, we must deliver:

- Flexibility
- Cooperation
- Empathy
- Opportunity
- Recognition
- Reward

- Education
- Training
- Communication
- Participation
- Less commanding
- More collaborating

Many small business owners fall into the trap of thinking it's all about money. If they can't pay as much as the next guy, they'll be stuck with the leftovers. In a study conducted by Randstand Staffing, two-thirds of employers (there's that two-thirds number again) surveyed believed their employees would choose more money over the opportunity to work at least some days at home. However, when the *employees* were surveyed, only half of them said they would choose the money. The other half would prefer the flexible work arrangements. If you think about it, their answer is a statement that time is becoming increasingly more important than money. This trend had already begun prior to this decade, but following the events of September 11, 2001, the trend has become even more pronounced.

An Expedia survey found that one in four employees would take a pay cut to have more time off. As you go up the management ladder, the desire for more time off rather than more money increases. In a survey sponsored by Hilton Hotels, 65 percent of the participants (again, two-thirds) said that they would be willing to take less pay to get more time off.

It's not just a choice between time and money, of course. In a CareerBuilder survey, 45 percent of workers were dissatisfied with the opportunities for career advancement within their own organization.

As a small business owner who wants to grow your business, you need to be clear on the advantages you have to offer.

What can you do that a big company cannot? What can you do that will attract winners to your organization?

YOU'RE ALWAYS RECRUITING

Most small business owners I've observed see hiring as an unpleasant chore. It's a to-do list task to be squeezed in between other more important duties. I hear them say things such as, "Man, you've got to kiss a lot of frogs to find the person you're looking for," or "I can't be wasting time in all those interviews." The worst one is, "In my town, you just can't find enough people who want to work." You can talk to an owner in Buffalo or Boise and get the same lament.

My friend Charlie Wonderlic, president of Wonderlic, Inc., knows more about small business hiring and training than anyone I know. His company is not only a privately held, fast-growth company but also a leader in helping employers hire and retain the best people. "In too many privately held companies, more time and effort is spent evaluating the cost and benefits of a new copy machine than a new employee," explains Wonderlic. "Equipment purchases are always based on a thorough analysis of features, functionality, price, and return on investment. Hiring decisions are typically made based more on 'gut feelings.' Think about it—which is the bigger investment?"

In most cases, these business owners have waited until they're desperate for help. They then throw out a quick classified ad on Monster.com or in their local paper and have an assistant sort through 50 resumes to find the best 10. The manager then interviews three and hires the first person who looks as though he or she can do the job without screwing up too much. These business owners just want to fill the position so they can "get back to their real job."

Guess what—it just doesn't work that way. Hiring the best and the brightest should never be an event prompted by a recent transition or growth spurt. You need to be in hiring mode every week of the year. It doesn't keep you from your job. This *is* your job.

For example, the finest manager I ever hired was a gentleman named Scott Hall. Scott was the plant manager of VF Corporation's Lee Jeans manufacturing facility in Jasper, Georgia. When I first met Scott, he was managing hundreds of people. I knew I would eventually need someone of Scott's caliber, but I didn't know when that time would come.

Years before the company could justify or afford Scott, we began the process of wooing him. I asked him first to a friendly lunch just to get acquainted. At that point, I made no mention of being interested in someday hiring him. A few months later, I had him visit our small but growing organization. At that time, this 20-operator cut-and-sew operation must have appeared quaint to this big-time operational expert. You can imagine his surprise when I eventually confessed that I had designs on one day hiring him to lead our production team.

It took a couple more years for us to build the critical mass to interest Scott. Once we could justify hiring him, he still rebuffed our interest on more than one occasion. But persistence paid off, and Scott became the key hire in an organization that grew from $2 million to $12 million in revenue during his six-year tenure. Looking back on it now, hiring Scott was more important than any marketing or financial decision we made.

I knew Scott was good. I now know he is the finest manager I've ever worked beside. He taught me more about what it means to be an outstanding manager than any class or any book I've ever read. It may interest you to know that Scott has now gone on to be a successful business owner himself, building a successful, 40-employee cut-and-sew operation in the north Georgia hills at a time when apparel manufacturing has all but died in this country.

The Scott Halls of the world are few and far between, but they are out there and it is your job to find them. You can't wait until you need a Scott Hall before you start looking. The chances of having an all-star employee's availability coincide with your own opportunity are miniscule. You need to be building a database of outstanding people and continually forging relationships with them to better your odds.

Dave Anderson, author of the book *Up Your Business* (Hoboken, NJ: Wiley, 2003), advises growing companies to print "eagle cards" that everyone in the organization hands out to top performers they meet in all walks of life. Anyone who brings in a star who is hired receives a bonus. The card is a recruiting advertisement, spelling out what kind of star performers the company is looking for, with a manager's direct telephone number listed for follow-up. "As desperation rises, standards fall," Anderson says. "If you want to hire great people, you'd better be prepared to go hire them yourself. You must go from waiting to be hunted to being a hunter."

One of the best ways to have a ready stable of great candidates is to cast a wide net. As technology has allowed human resources personnel to sift resumes by keyword, job descriptions and resumes have gotten more and more specialized. It has reached a point where savvy job applicants game the system by customizing every single resume they send out. When all goes well, the company gets to hire someone with exactly the right experience for very specific requirements. But is that person really the best candidate? Could someone with a different perspective add more to the job and have more upside potential in the future? Could someone who is at the top of his or her game in another industry help you open new markets or develop new approaches?

I am continually amazed at how specific some job advertisements have become. In sales, for example, I have seen successful salespeople move effortlessly among selling advertising, software, and consulting services. Yet, when I see advertisements for salespeople, they often limit themselves to a tiny sliver of the labor pool. One ad I saw recently was looking for someone with "at least 10 years' experience in selling corrugated cardboard products in the Southeast." I don't mean to belittle this industry, but isn't it possible to train a top sales performer on the ins and outs of selling cardboard?

Another ad was looking for "a proven sales leader who has brought in at least $500K per year in revenue for the last five years selling hand-held power tools." Why run an ad at all for this narrow specification? The company should already know who fits this description. If those stars aren't already on the manager's radar, the company should hire a headhunter to call the handful of people who qualify and offer them a job. Better yet, hire someone who has proven over and over that he or she can deliver in any market and train the person well in your product or service category.

Unfortunately, I see this quest for superspecialization across industries and across job functions. I'd love to have a dollar for every time someone has said to me, "Our industry is different" or "You don't understand how things work in the gizmo business." No, I don't know the intricacies of your industry, but neither did you at one time. Neither did most of your best employees or the best employees of your competitor. Industries and day-to-day job functions can be learned. Talent and brains cannot. Cast a wide net for talent and brains—the industry-specific knowledge can be taught over time.

SLOW TO HIRE . . .

In too many privately held companies, hiring is a sprint. There's a loud and abrupt start, a flurry of activity, and lots of heavy breathing at the finish line. If you blink, you miss it. My advice is that you think of hiring more like a marathon. Your starting position is ill defined and has little effect on the eventual outcome. A slow and steady rhythm is the winning technique. I've never seen a winning marathoner who sprints for a mile and then rests to catch his breath before sprinting again. Have you ever noticed that, be it track and field, bicycling, or swimming, it's the long-distance athletes that appear less out of breath than the sprinters? When you are doing it right, your hiring practices should look like an endurance event: a slow, steady, rhythmic effort.

Most growth companies look at hiring as one of their highest priorities, if not *the* highest. A group of top managers interviews the candidates in shifts, in detail. Everyone asks probing questions and takes notes. The managers frame questions that address the company's core values or sense of purpose. The group meets at a set time to compare impressions (based on substance, not clothing and hairstyles) and discuss results.

The best performers are asking the questions because the company wants more people like them, not more people like the average. Average managers hire average employees, probably ones who are not too threatening and will do what they are told. Peak performers strive to hire more people like themselves—superstars who can grow the business.

It's So Hard to Find Good People These Days!

I was recently sitting in a hotel lobby in a growing city of more than 1 million people. I couldn't help but overhear a conversation between two business owners who were both obviously struggling in general. Everything was wrong for these guys—the economy, the government, pricing pressures, and so on. You name it, these guys had a problem with it. But without question, their biggest problem of all was their inability, in their minds, to find "people who want to work." Both agreed it was their number one issue. Given their pessimistic tone, I have no doubt it will stay that way.

Contrast these perceived problems with the experience of my friends at PrintingForLess.com, based in Livingston, Montana, with a population of just over 7,000. Montana is in the nation's fourth-largest state by area, but 48th in terms of population. You would have to drive hundreds of miles to reach a city where the population even approaches 200,000.

When PrintingForLess.com began, founder and president Andrew Field and a staff of five key employees knew they could grow only with highly skilled people. Initially, the fledgling organization looked outside its geography for expertise and experience. Electronic prepress managers and technicians and experienced press operators were recruited from as close as Seattle (700 miles) and as far away as upstate New York (2,000 miles). "We didn't have the time or infrastructure to train people at first, so we needed to hire people with industry experience who could hit the ground running," founder Field explains. "But we always knew that eventually we would have to train the local workforce if we wanted to grow."

Those initial out-of-state hires not only brought the PrintingForLess.com operation up to speed but also created the

(Continued)

(Continued)

foundation for a world-class recruitment and training program. Their target is young, bright, and energetic locals who know little to nothing about commercial printing.

The interview process is arduous. "You end up investing 8 or 10 hours of your life trying to get a job here," Field explains. "We interview extensively and are trying to determine customer service ability, whether the person is a good fit for our culture, and whether the candidate has future management potential." Apart from the actual interviews, the company administers extensive personality and problem-solving tests. "We hand candidates a project to complete, using an off-the-shelf software product that's unrelated to the printing industry. We watch how quickly they figure it out. Is the technical challenge intuitive for them, or are they struggling?"

PrintingForLess.com now has more than 100 well-trained, motivated, and loyal employees. It's the critical component of their growth. Other well-funded attempts at online commercial printing have proven unsuccessful over the years because they forgot that people matter most. Sure, PrintingForLess.com's web-based customer interface was a stroke of genius, and certainly their customer-driven internal processes would be the envy of any world-class operation. But founder Field and his management team never lose sight of what really brings success. As Field explains, "The key thing is that no matter how badly you need to get people hired, you can't afford to get lax in your standards. Great people bring our business growth."

By the way, PrintingForLess.com's operations are so unique, they now prefer to hire people with no experience. "We have a bias against industry experience now," Field explains. "We do things so differently here, we find that people with printing experience have to unlearn what they knew before."

References are checked. Past claims are verified. If the top candidate was a referral from an employee, that source is also tapped for information. Once a candidate is chosen, someone extends an offer, reiterates the company's core values, and sends out a formal employment offer. This process may take a couple of weeks. Growing companies may be in dire need of bodies, but they should not sacrifice quality for expediency. They are slow to hire.

This doesn't mean that if a superstar is suddenly available, the company will twiddle their thumbs and hold multiple interviews. If top managers have been actively recruiting, the "checking out the candidate" phase will already be done. They are still slow to hire, but the evaluation is already finished. In the ideal situation, there is some kind of superstar file somewhere, with background information enclosed for each potential recruit.

In any case, the interview is the ideal time to introduce your core values or sense of purpose. The candidate will benefit because he or she will be able to determine whether the company is a good fit. The company will benefit because the interviewer can see how the candidate reacts to those values and be sure the person knows what he or she is getting into. Try to frame questions in a way that can measure your mutual compatibility.

YOU CAN'T TRAIN FOR BRAIN, BUT YOU CAN TEST FOR THE BEST

I can't train a person to be smart. Conversely, I can train a smart person to do most anything. When it comes to hiring, innate intelligence, as measured by problem-solving ability, should be your common denominator. Whether you are hiring a third-shift machine operator or high-level financial analyst, that person should be at the highest range possible in his or her particular job category. Nothing is a better predictor of success in the position than this.

The preceding sentence probably rubbed you the wrong way. You won't find a statement like this in a feel-good *Reader's Digest* human interest story. American mythology is filled with stories of people who overcome apparent deficiencies. So, it's practically un-American for me to suggest that hard work, experience, and a "can-do attitude" can't overcome a lack of mental acuity. Believe me, I know. Nothing elicits a more visceral response in my speeches than this very topic. Frankly, I don't even enjoy telling you this cold, hard truth. No employee can be trained to be intelligent. You cannot make people smart; they simply are or they are not.

I know of one former small business in the technology field that took the "can't train for brain" attitude to a successful extreme. From the first days of TCS Management's inception, founder Jim Gordon had only one rule on who could be hired: Each person had to have graduated from a four-year college. All else being equal, the candidate who had graduated with honors would win out over one who hadn't. For engineering positions, a specialized education or extensive experience was expected. For other positions, however, he didn't care whether applicants had a degree in Spanish literature, sports medicine, or art history. He just wanted proof that the people could apply themselves, learn, and accomplish something that took a lot of work. The company's extensive training program ensured that specialized industry knowledge would come in time.

The company quickly became the undisputed growth leader in its call center software niche. Turnover was unusually low. Job advertisements were rarely run because most new hires were employee referrals. After a decade of continuous growth, a larger technology partner purchased the company for an obscene sum.

In an earlier chapter, I emphasized the importance of training—the right training. If people don't know what the company's core reason for being is and what the organization is trying to accomplish, they are not going to be able to do their best. However, this assumes that you have the right people in the right positions. All the training in the world isn't going to turn a lousy people person into your best customer service rep. Someone who is terrible at math is not going to make a good financial manager, no matter how much training he or she gets.

Part of the reason you should be slow to hire is that you should take the time to test candidates for their proficiency. Testing determines whether you are hiring the right person for the job or taking a chance. Testing tells you if you are putting talented candidates in a position that won't make the best use of their talents.

Testing can be formal when a specific skill is involved: technical positions, accounting positions, or IT positions. Certifications may take the place of formal testing, but candidates should still be verbally questioned by someone in the know to make sure that what was covered in the certificate program really sank in. Likewise, 20 years of experience does not automatically mean that people know what you want them to know. By testing their knowledge, you can be sure.

. . . QUICK TO FIRE

Let's say you've now done everything right in the hiring process. You've kissed a lot of frogs. You've run all the tests, checked all the references, and finally pulled the trigger. The offer has been tendered and accepted. Everyone is happy, the birds are chirping, the sun is shining, and all is right with the world.

Sometimes, however, despite our best efforts, we come to realize we've made a mistake. Maybe it's just a little mistake. Maybe it's a huge mistake. Either way, I know I've made a mistake within the new hire's first two weeks. When I suggest this two-week notion to any group of business owners, it always elicits a hearty chuckle. Then I drop the real punch line: "If we know we have made a mistake in the first two weeks, why do we let the situation fester for two years?" That's what draws the biggest laugh, because everyone has been in those shoes.

Why do we take so long to rectify the situation? There are undoubtedly countless reasons. One, we can't face running another marathon after having just finished one. Perhaps we feel guilty to have brought someone in from out of town or because we had that person quit another job to join our organization. We hope against hope that we can improve the situation over time and that the problem will eventually take care of itself through behavior modification efforts or attrition. But really, the primary reason we wait so long to take action is that it is difficult to admit to ourselves and to the rest of the organization we have made a mistake. Too often, we let our ego get in the way, and that's an even bigger mistake.

Ladies and gentlemen, let me be clear about this. Just as you have to be slow to hire, you need to adopt a philosophy of "quick to fire." Allowing a bad seed to germinate in your orchard can destroy your entire crop. Tolerating poor performers reinforces an idea that you accept mediocrity. That's a sure way to scare off your superstars. The best and brightest want to win, and they want to work in a place filled with people like themselves. If you don't foster that environment, they'll find a place that does.

Once you have identified that you have made a hiring mistake, it is imperative that you act quickly and decisively. You owe it to yourself and to the dedicated staff you have worked so hard to attract. You even owe it to this new hire. If someone is not right for your organization, you are doing that person no favor by keeping him or her in the fold. The quicker you let such people go, the quicker they can move on with the rest of their lives and the easier it will be for them to explain the situation in subsequent interviews. If you need to give them a generous severance to make the transition easier, then so be it. I'm not so Machiavellian as to suggest you don't owe the person something for your mistake. What I am suggesting is that you can't let emotion play any role in this action. Just get it done.

This may sound heartless, but doing otherwise is a sure way to stall growth. If you want to build a growing business, you can't do it alone. You also can't do it on the backs of a few stars who have to carry everyone else. You cannot afford average, much less poor, performance. If you're going to win, you need winners. In the end, I would rather you err on the side of action than take a wait-and-see attitude. If you know in your gut you've got a problem, then you do. I'm simply suggesting you take care of it sooner rather than later.

YOU CAN'T ALWAYS DANCE WITH THE ONE THAT BRUNG YA

One of the most difficult aspects of small business growth is the day you realize you've outgrown a long-term employee. Maybe he has not kept up his skill sets. Perhaps the rate of change has left him bewildered, causing him to long for the good ole days, "when this place used to run right." I have one consulting client, who has asked to remain anonymous, who has a real problem between the old guard and the newbies. This year, that company will hire more new people than they had total employees three years ago. Some of the old guard embrace this rapid rate of growth and change, while others block change at every turn. You can never anticipate who will grow with you and who will fight change. All you can do is continually monitor the situation for potential trouble.

GE popularized the approach of continually evaluating all employees, ranking them, and then getting rid of the bottom performers in each business unit. Some have called the strategy cruel and inflexible, while others have hailed it as the greatest idea in the history of human resources and adopted the process wholesale. I would suggest that a middle ground is probably appropriate for most private business owners. If the entire sales department is giving 110 percent and everyone is pulling his or her weight, it is ridiculous to apply some ranking that forces someone in that group to be penalized. If the whole shipping department missed their goals by 50 percent and everyone there is equally at fault, there's no point in rewarding the best of the bad. It is probably time to bring in a whole new team.

The honest truth is that some people don't want to be challenged. They don't want to be part of a company that demands peak performance and is constantly changing. They would rather work in a predictable job for a predictable company and collect a predictable paycheck. Some companies may need people like that, but you don't. If you really want to grow and grow successfully, you can't keep people who want to stand still or who are pining for "the good ole days." They simply don't belong in a growth organization.

If your revenues are half a million dollars a year and you grow by 20 percent, you've added $100,000 in revenue. In my former companies, that would mean one or possibly two new hires. But what about when you're at $10 million in revenue and you experience 20 percent growth, which means adding $2 million in revenue? This probably means 20 new employees and probably a new senior manager or two to boot. It's a sad but true fact that the employee who can withstand 20 percent growth in your early stages is not necessarily equipped to handle 20 percent or more growth on down the line.

COMMUNICATE, EVALUATE, AND REWARD

Hiring is just the beginning. Just as customer acquisition is the first step toward building greater lifetime value, so, too, is hiring the beginning of a mutually beneficial relationship. From the day new hires walk through your doors, they want to feel valued and feel that their contribution matters. Employees' first day sets the tone for their whole tenure with you. If nobody has time to spend with them, if nothing they need to get started is ready, or if they are hurriedly introduced to 30 people in the first hour and then left to fill out paperwork, what kind of impression are they going to have? What are they going to tell the spouse or best friend who asks, "How was your first day?" You want the answer to be, "This is going to be the best opportunity I ever had!" What you can't afford are answers like, "Well, they didn't have a computer ready for me yet, but they promised it would be ready by the end of the week. I think they might have forgotten I was coming." Devise a plan for the way new employees will be integrated into the company culture, and make sure it is someone's top priority for the day, or better yet, the week.

Next, schedule a follow-up conversation for a few weeks after their first day. Ideally, new hires should be meeting with their immediate supervisor, the department manager, and the head honcho. All of these people should be probing, asking for feedback, and figuring out what has gone well and what hasn't. New hires' "fresh eyes" provide valuable feedback. This is also an ideal time to make sure new employees understand the company's core values and what it is trying to accomplish.

Then, on a regular schedule, these employees are coached and evaluated. They know what goals they are trying to hit and how they will be measured. They also know that if they hit their goals, they will be rewarded. If they continually fall short, there will be consequences. They know there will be regularly scheduled communication sessions and that they are free to voice concerns or offer ideas in the meantime. They know that innovation and creativity are rewarded, provided they further the goals everyone knows by heart. The simplest way to do that is to say, "Here's where we should be in six months. How do we get there?" Make it clear why it needs to happen and what people will reap personally if the goals are achieved.

If you have done your job right, your business will hum like a well-oiled machine, whether you are in the office or not. If you ask any employee where the company is headed, he or she will be able to tell you. He or she will not be wondering, "What's in it for me?"

DON'T DO—DELEGATE

Once you hire the best and the brightest, set a course and get out of the way. Next time you see a successful business owner you admire somewhere outside his or her office, a leader who has attained the level of growth for which you strive, I'd be willing to bet that person appears relaxed and in control. He or she won't appear to be harried by endless interruptions and fires needing his or her attention. For instance, I am continually amazed by how easy it is to reach the president of fast-growth companies by phone. It's the *struggling* entrepreneur who is too busy to talk to anyone. Fast-growth leaders are not micromanaging things back at the shop because they know they have the right people in place to take care of the day-to-day business. Every phone call they make has an impact. They leverage their time in ways that will get the biggest return, with most of it spent on developing key people and taking the time to regularly consider the future.

You are probably familiar with the Pareto Principle, commonly known as the 80/20 rule. It suggests, for example, that 80 percent of your revenue comes from 20 percent of your customers and that 80 percent of your profit comes from 20 percent of your products or services offered. The numbers are not absolute, but the general principle is amazingly accurate across a variety of functions. The best leaders know that it also applies to time management. They know that 80 percent of their results come from 20 percent of their activities. So, that crucial 20 percent is always at the top of the priority list. Spend your time on what really matters, not on what "needs to get done." You'll never cross everything off your to-do list, but if you properly leverage a great team, you can cross off the items that have the highest impact.

Entrepreneurs by nature tend to be individualistic and confident. They trust their instincts and are willing to take risks when it makes sense. For a while, many of them are able to grow their companies through hard work, boundless energy, and strong salesmanship. They start to believe they can accomplish anything if they can just find enough hours in the day.

As their business grows, however, they often have trouble letting go of key functions and start to hit snags. Over time, the businesses stall and the owners wonder what went wrong. They ask themselves: "I'm working harder than ever—why is it getting so difficult to keep growing?" In most cases, the owner's best move would be to hire people smarter than himself or herself. Communicate the goals; then let the people do their jobs. Working half as many hours, the business owner with a strong team will likely get twice the results.

An effective leader can go on vacation for two weeks or more and truly enjoy it. Why not? Such a leader has hammered home the core values and has established well-defined goals for each manager. Most importantly, he or she has put a great team in place and has given people the latitude to make the right decisions without calling the business owner first. If the owner of a growing company who is on vacation has to call in every set break from her mixed doubles set, she has failed as a leader.

Consider Ted Turner, the quintessential fast-growth entrepreneur. Have you ever wondered how ol' Ted managed to lead his organization through its staggering growth, while simultaneously finding the time to win yachting races? When Ted Turner won the America's Cup in 1977, he was running Turner Broadcasting and owned the Atlanta Braves and Atlanta Hawks. Throughout the launch of CNN in 1980, he was still racing boats and trying to recapture the Cup crown.

Yvon Chouinard, the founder of adventure gear catalog Patagonia, worked in the company headquarters for only six months a year. The rest of the year he was off climbing other mountains—literally. Their first mail order piece stated, "Don't expect speedy delivery in the [prime climbing] months of May, June, July, August and September." Chouinard continued to climb mountains around the world as Patagonia became an Inc. 500 winner and a household name.

Richard Branson's worldwide Virgin brands were never built while he sat in an office. Even while he was establishing Virgin Atlantic Airways, opening music superstores, and signing bands to his record label in the 1980s and 1990s, he was setting records in his hot air balloon and speedboat.

FIND THE BEST SUPPLIERS, PARTNERS, AND CUSTOMERS

One last note about having the best people on board: Small business owners and managers should not stop at the hiring function when looking for the best and brightest. People are attracted to winners. They want to associate with the best. You also need to link up with the best people when looking for suppliers, partners, and even customers. You want top-notch companies sending you supplies, sending you customers, and helping you get your marketing message out. You want the best customers buying from you because you know they value what you have to offer. If they are satisfied, they will spread the word to more good customers.

One of the best ways I know to grow your business is to align yourself with organizations that think the same way you do, not necessarily the ones with the biggest purchase orders today.

SUGGESTED NEXT STEPS

1. If you currently have employees, make an honest assessment of their skills and talents. Ask yourself if this group of people can get you to the next level.

2. If you have no employees, ask yourself what must happen to allow you to start hiring the best and brightest.

3. Find an easy to administer test for problem-solving ability that you can use to test for the best. I like Wonderlic products and services (www.wonderlic.com), but there are others.

4. Make a list of the 10 or more standouts in your industry and geography you wish you could hire. Start a dialog ASAP.

5. Design a detailed first week for a new hire. Be sure it instills a lasting impression of opportunity and excitement.

9

RULE 7:
SEE THE FUTURE
MORE CLEARLY

. . . those who look only to the past or present are certain to miss the future.

—John F. Kennedy

Despite man's best efforts and greatest inventions, we simply cannot predict the future.

But that simple truism hasn't stopped us from trying. It's a frustration that has confounded great thinkers and leaders since the dawn of civilization. While we can't predict the future, the desire to make predictions can be characterized as a fundamental human trait. Why do we do it?

There are probably plenty of psychological and spiritual reasons that human beings feel compelled to foretell the future. These things are clearly outside my realm of expertise. But in the world of industry and commerce, I think the reason is pretty obvious. We've all witnessed how success can come to those who appear to see the future more clearly than others. From ancient fishermen's attempt at weather prediction, to more modern prognostications in the stock market, man's commercial endeavors have also recognized the value in being able to anticipate. No, we can't predict the future, but some can envision the future to a useful degree of accuracy.

For example, Las Vegas oddsmakers can't accurately predict the outcome of a specific game; they just do it a little better than most of us over the course of many games. Insurance companies are in a similar business. Sometimes they take too much risk, sometimes not enough, but they've usually got their bets covered, so to speak. The house always wins. Agricultural products, energy futures, and hotel pricing systems work in much the same way. They all deal in future probabilities, based on calculable trends from the past and the measurable conditions of the present. They also have size on their side. These are big enough markets and companies that they can spread their exposure out pretty evenly. Sometimes they lose big (like Lloyds of London recently) but not very often.

Small business owners are usually thought of as risk-takers. In Chapter 2, I tried to dispel that myth to an extent. Here, however, I think the description is more apt. Small business is inherently a greater risk than big business in terms of covering our bets. While size can be among our strengths in some areas, we *are* more susceptible to the fickle nature of fate due to size. Small businesses are more dependent on a few key people, a few primary products, or a few key suppliers. There are many qualitative aspects to small business that could significantly influence our long-term prospects for success, as opposed to the relatively straightforward quantitative models used in things such as actuary tables and sports books. Sports books would never bet everything on a single team. You do it every day.

Banks have gotten better at addressing small business risk, for example, by bundling our debt service agreements together with other small businesses. However, to grow more wisely, it is also incumbent on us to recognize our inherent risk exposure and to do something to lower it. The best way I know for a small business owner like you to mitigate risk is to take the time to regularly consider the macroforces of change and their impact on your business, industry, and community. From that effort, you then must make bold and specific predictions about the future. I'm not suggesting tea leaves or tarot cards. I am suggesting that you become an expert on how the future will impact your business. I am also suggesting that this is a common characteristic among successful entrepreneurs: the ability to see the future more clearly than others. It's a skill that anyone interested in growth must develop, especially in today's turbulent marketplace.

THE ACCIDENTAL FUTURIST

No educator thinks twice about the need to study history. To some students, like me, it's interesting; to others, a source of inspiration or wisdom; to most, a necessary tedium. You've no doubt heard the famous warning, "Those who fail to study history are doomed to repeat it," attributed to many over the years. I think George Bernard Shaw put it better when he said, "We learn from history that we learn nothing from history." Either way, history has been taught at all levels of education for eons. Most people think that's a good idea, and I concur. History teaches us valuable lessons about who we are and where we come from.

What I don't understand is why we don't place the same emphasis on the future. If it's a basic human drive and important in so many ways to our sense of well-being, why aren't we taught more about the future—not just what the future may hold, but how we might go about making those forecasts our-selves? In most cases, we are not taught how to see the future.

So, what can you do to bring the future into better focus?

MONITOR ONGOING CHANGE

The place to start is with your own internal history. Find ways to record and measure the most meaningful growth indica-tors within your organization. These leading indicators vary from industry to industry and company to company. In busi-nesses I've managed, we always looked to establish ongoing trend lines for the number of new customers, average order size, lifetime customer values, overall sales growth, and sales within specific segmentation categories (geography, type of business, etc.).

I now recommend the same indicators to my clients, in ad-dition to those metrics specific to their industry. Most of my growth friends from PrintingForLess.com to Candlewic use these indicators *every day* to manage their growth. And here's the great thing: It never ceases to amaze me how good you can get at forecasting when working with accurate historical data. On the whole, in general terms, growth patterns for most businesses are predictable in terms that are useful. In other words, we can't get it right on the nose, but we can use trend lines to help us get a glimpse into our future.

In Chapter 4, I suggested that the well-informed growth leader read 50 magazines a month to stay current. But I'm not hung up on magazines. Books, web sites, secondary re-search and reports, speeches, and newspapers are all valuable change-monitoring tools. The disciplined gathering of data from many sources is called *scanning* by futurists, and it's the way in which they begin to "predict" the future. All they're really doing is identifying and monitoring ongoing patterns of change. They are also looking to connect the dots between seemingly disparate pieces of information, trying to find emerging issues and trends. Scanning also helps us identify the all-important "weak signals" that sit on the periphery of our businesses, our industries, and our lives, but can have the most far-reaching effect. (See Uncle O and the Weak Signals Band.)

Anyone can hone his or her change-monitoring skills, given enough time and effort. However, growth leaders in small business are often naturals at this. They don't usually know that's what they're doing, but they are often expert change monitors nonetheless. Most successful, growth-oriented entrepreneurs I know are voracious gatherers of information. By combining their own internal trend data, their external scanning efforts, and an understanding of potentially disruptive weak signals, they are prepared to take their forecasting to the next level.

CONSIDER IMPACTS

To see the future more clearly, it's not enough to simply gather the data revolving around change. At some point, uncovering emerging issues and calculating ongoing trends lead us to consider the importance of the change. Will the change significantly impact our industry or product/service category? If so, in what ways will the change potentially manifest itself? In what ways is the change a threat? An opportunity?

Small businesses often make the mistake of being too narrow when considering the potential impact of change. They tend to side with the easiest to imagine or most prevailing thinking within their organizations or industries. Some people call this *group-think,* and it's to be avoided at all costs.

For example, I was recently asked to speak to a trade association involved in commercial construction. The conference was made up of 300 or so owners and senior managers of

Uncle O and the Weak Signals Band

My wife's Uncle O, as we called him, recently passed away. Uncle O was in the music recording industry for his entire career. He started out as a small label owner and eventually became president of one of the world's largest recording labels. He had successfully navigated the turbulent and confusing world of pop music from the late 1950s through the early 1990s. In the two years before he died, I spent considerable time with Uncle O.

A fanatical fan of popular music ever since I bought my first Beatles single at age 3 ("Love Love Me Do" backed with "P.S. I Love You"), I could talk with Uncle O for hours about his insider's knowledge. While he had many compelling stories to share, I became most interested in understanding his uncanny ability to capitalize on the rapid rate of change in his industry. As much as any industry I know, the recorded music business is made up of seemingly well-entrenched "status quos" that are overthrown on a regular basis by the latest incarnation of "new."

Consider the rapid rate of change in Uncle O's industry. Everything—from the industry's distribution systems to the media formats sold to the styles of music people buy—changes quickly and completely. In fact, the only thing that stays consistent is the rapid rate of change. Uncle O maintained that his success stemmed from an ability to see the periphery of a changing market more clearly than his competition.

Though he never used the term, Uncle O was an early practitioner of what some call *weak signal* monitoring. Weak signals are outliers: ideas and products and styles that lie on the fringe of awareness. Here are a few rules of weak signals that I learned from listening to Uncle O:

(Continued)

- The more irreverent and upsetting a new idea is to the status quo, the more chance it has of reaching a level of importance.
- The more often you hear, "That's just a fad," the more likely it's not.
- Identifying and monitoring weak signals should be an on-going, systematic process.
- The ability to see the next big thing before it happens is equal parts art and science.
- Weak signals often grow by joining forces with other weak signals. In other words, weak signals often need reinforcement from other ideas floating outside the established boundaries before they can be seen or heard.

As a manager and a business leader, Uncle O believed his focus should be on the future. He estimated that, in his most productive periods, he was spending 75 percent of his time on identifying, monitoring, developing, and retooling initiatives designed to meet tomorrow's opportunities. Managing the day-to-day activities of today's opportunity was something he could delegate with confidence.

It is interesting that most small business owners spend the majority of their time on today's issues (or even yesterday's issues), while managers of growth organizations have their gaze firmly fixed on tomorrow. To Uncle O, managing a current hit was relatively easy. Attempting to identify the next big thing is where he brought the most value to his organization.

organizations which built large office buildings. A few were from publicly held companies, but most were smaller, privately held businesses. The conference organizers asked me to speak about growth and the future of opportunity in the commercial construction industry.

Admittedly, I am not a commercial construction expert. In fact, I don't even own a tool belt. However, I am a pretty quick study. I set about preparing myself to discuss the future of the office space. I investigated everything I could about the big macroforces of change within the industry. I considered the social, political, technological, economic, and environmental trends that might impact commercial construction. I honed in on one major change that I thought might have a significant impact on the office space: the "grayification" of the average American worker—the fact that the age of the average American worker continues to increase and the trend is likely to continue.

After forming my own list of potential impacts on the grayification trend, I asked my 13-year-old son the following question: "If the average age of the American worker is getting increasingly older, how do you think it will affect the typical office building in the future?" He envisioned a workspace with ubiquitous wheelchair access and a central nurses' station on each level in case the decrepit needed a jump start. His answer was both logical and familiar, as I had read similar prognostications in the industry's trade publications and academic journals. I had a hunch my audience expected me to elaborate on this specific future vision.

The only problem was that I didn't share this view. In fact, for me, this scenario misses the whole point. My son can be forgiven for his overly simplistic view. He is 13 and, despite getting straight A's last semester, knows relatively little about commercial construction. I couldn't say the same for some commercial construction pundits I was reading.

The real shift here is not that there are more old people. Instead, the very idea of *what it means to be old is shifting*. The primary reason our population is increasingly older is that technology allows us to stay healthier and stronger, not sicker and weaker. When Ronald Reagan turned 80 while in office, it was a harbinger of many things to come in our society, but that didn't include more wheelchairs and nurses in the White House. Aging boomers already report that they will want to work for as long as they physically can (which is a good thing given their paltry rate of savings). While they will be increasingly interested in building safety and comfort (who isn't?), they won't want or need work space that resembles a retirement community. In fact, I anticipate that they'll go to great lengths to avoid anything that smacks of "senior." What 60 meant to my grandfather will be what 85 will mean to my son.

Will I be right on all this? Who knows? The point is you shouldn't listen to me or any other so-called expert. When it comes to the specifics of how macrochanges like demographics will affect your industry or company, you need to weigh the various potential impacts emanating from that change. What is the most likely scenario? Are there other plausible scenarios? How likely are they to occur?

DEVELOP A RESPONSE

After monitoring change and considering the impact of those changes, it's important to ultimately develop an appropriate response. The future is anything but a foregone conclusion, and growth-centric entrepreneurs specialize in making choices and taking actions that shape their future. The future isn't something that happens to them; it happens because of them. They use their analytical and intuitive skills to develop a plan of action in response to the synthesis of their knowledge. The better they are at turning their foresight into informed action, the better they are at sustainable growth.

I can't tell you what your response should be to the macro-forces of change that surround you. That's for you to decide. What I can suggest is a systematic and regular effort to insert the future into your ongoing planning efforts. An organization's ability to put the future into the plan with any degree of accuracy is rare. The ability to take action on such a plan is where the money is made.

THE FUTURE AIN'T WHAT IT USED TO BE

A new factor, that of rapid change, has come into the world. We have not yet learned how to adjust ourselves to its economic and social consequences.

—Wallace B. Dohham, *Harvard Business Review*

I use this quote in many of my speeches. I ask the audience if it accurately describes how they currently feel. Most everyone raises his or her hand. Nearly all think they are having trouble keeping up with the rate of change in their business and personal life. The funny thing is, this quote is from 1932. In 1932, we felt powerless against the onslaught of social, technological, economic, and political change. Is it no wonder we feel a little uncomfortable today?

In the following sections, I give you a head start on what I consider to be some of the most important macrotrends that are certain to affect you and your business. Understanding these forces a little better should help you more clearly see your business future.

Shifting Demographics

Without question, the most important macrochange happening in our world today is the dramatic shift in demographics.

We, as human beings, are fundamentally and rapidly changing forever. Consider these trends:

- In 1900, 12 percent of the world's population lived in cities. Today, that number is roughly half. Twenty years from now, that number will be 62 percent. There are now more than 400 cities in the world with populations over 1 million. In 1900, there were 13.
- If we were to put together a list of everyone in the history of the human race who has ever been over the age of 65, two-thirds of those people would be alive today. (Go back and read that one again. It's a biggie.)
- The grayification of the industrialized world (the average age in Japan, Germany, and Italy will be over 50 in 30 years) is in sharp contrast to the increasingly youthful populations of developing nations in Africa and the Middle East, where the average age is invariably under 20.
- At the same time that much of the world is moving into urban areas, Americans are increasing their rate of urban decentralization, with terms such as *sprawl* and *exurbia* now part of our everyday lexicon. The U.S. Census Bureau found that more Americans moved out of metropolitan areas between 1995 and 2000 than moved in.
- Americans are becoming more culturally and ethnically diverse. Currently, 10 percent of Americans are foreign born. The United States is now the second largest Spanish-speaking nation in the world and the largest market for Spanish-language music. In Los Angeles County, California, minorities own 40 percent of small businesses.
- Diversity is spreading. The state with the fastest growing Hispanic population is not California, Texas, or Florida—it's North Carolina. More than 5,000 Kurds are now living in Nashville, Tennessee. Thousands of Hmong people

from the northern mountains of Southeast Asia are now living in Wisconsin and Minnesota. According to the 2000 U.S. Census, there are also 41 other Asian nationalities in Minnesota. Four of the top 10 languages spoken in the United States are now Asian. In just the state of Virginia, there are more than 20,000 residents who speak each of the following languages: Hindi, Arabic, Tagalog, Korean, and Vietnamese.

• There are more people living in just China and India today than there were people living in the entire world at the end of WWII. However, most people don't realize that the actual rate of population growth has decreased significantly from its peak of 2.2 percent in 1970 to an estimated 1 percent by 2020. In other words, the rate of growth for world population will have decreased by more than 50 percent over a 50-year period.

China Changes Everything

I really do read 50 magazines a month. Rarely are they the same ones, but there are a few that I can't do without. I am often asked which one is the most important. I answer, without hesitation, *The Economist*. Since 1843, this London-based weekly has consistently delivered the most complete and thorough reporting on the state of the world from an economic and geopolitical viewpoint.

In the long tradition of English stoicism and understatement, *The Economist* is not given to hyperbole. That's why, when I read the following in the August 21, 2004, issue, I had to go back and read it a few times: "Since Deng Xiaoping launched his 'open door' policy in 1978, China has witnessed the most dramatic burst of wealth creation in the history of mankind."

Wow! Not Renaissance Italy, not post-WWII United States, but China. The article went on to explain that 400 million people (a population greater than the United States) have been lifted out of poverty in that time, income per person has risen sevenfold in the same period, and the economy will continue to grow between 7.9 percent and 9.2 percent in the coming years. Right now, China is growing in any way you would want to measure it:

- China is the most populated country in the world, with over 1.3 billion inhabitants, according to the United Nations World Population Database (2002 edition).
- In 2000, there were just over 5 million cars on the roads in China. By the end of 2005, that number will be 24 million, according to The Worldwatch Institute ("State of the World 2004, Special Focus: The Consumer Society," January 2004). Volkswagen already sells more cars in China than they do in Germany.
- China consumes over half of the world's pork, over half the world's concrete, 40 percent of the world's steel, and 33 percent of its polymers such as polypropylene.
- Historically, China has been a net exporter of grains. By 2005, China will be a net importer. By 2007, net grain imports are conservatively projected to be over 40 million metric tons. This is a swing of more than 60 million metric tons in just the past five years. For comparison, the entire exportable surplus of the United States in wheat and feed grain is only 80 million metric tons. Among the 10 fastest growing cities in the world between 1995 and 2005, half have been in China (Wenzhou, Yantai, Jinxi, Xuzhou, Nanchong). Even more interesting to me is the fact I had heard of only one of them.

I think you get the idea. China is big and getting bigger. More importantly, China will continue to affect you and your business. I say "continue to," because it already has to a large degree. For instance, there are many reasons we are paying more at the pump for gas, but China's insatiable and rising demand for oil is a primary culprit. There are very few businesses in this country that aren't impacted directly by higher gasoline prices. This is just the start. Imagine what demand for most things will look like in 10 years, when China's economy will have more than doubled.

When I share this dramatic information on China with business owners and leaders in the United States, there is a tendency for people to feel threatened. Change can be a threat, especially to those vested in the status quo. However, I prefer that you see these changes as representing incredible opportunity. For instance, the booming economy of China has created an enormous market for our goods and services. While China is relatively poor on a per capita basis in relation to Japan, the United States, and Western Europe, their consumer class of middle income purchasers is now second in size only to the United States. In my view, the Chinese glass is indeed half full.

How should you proceed with the giant impact and opportunities that China will create for your industry and your company? Here's my rule of thumb: If China needs more than they make, you will pay more for it. If China is making more than they need, you will pay less. Also, remember that the biggest impacts and opportunities are still to come. Right now, 60 percent of China's population is still involved in agriculture. What happens when they really set their sites on, say, technology?

Casper Technology

Technology has been, and will continue to be, the most visible force behind fundamental change in how you and I live. I've certainly tried to make that point throughout this book, and I recognize that I risk redundancy by mentioning it here again. So be it. It's that important. But let me offer a slightly new twist on the subject, because I believe that the very idea of technology, and how it intersects with our lives, is also about to undergo a revolution.

A couple of years ago, I participated in a two-day exercise in which people from all walks of life were asked to envision the ideal place to live and work in the near-term future. It was a fascinating exercise, full of crazy (good) ideas and real hope for a better way of life tomorrow. While there were many new concepts that emerged, the one that really stuck with me was the concept we coined *Casper technology*. Do you remember the old cartoon, "Casper, the Friendly Ghost"? The idea here was a friendly "ghost in the machine" that enhances our lives in simple, imperceptible, yet profound ways. I'm not talking about just information technology such as computers and cell phones. I'm talking about everything from bioengineering to nanotechnology to tall building architecture—friendlier, smarter technology that anticipates our needs, doesn't demand active participation, and steadily pushes us up the ladder toward true self-actualization.

We are still stuck with a mind-set that sees technology as having both limitations and benefits. We tend to view it as having produced as many deleterious effects as positive ones. Yes, the car gave us individual freedom, but it also is a big polluter and a leading cause of death among young people. Telecommunications has gotten so good that we can be found even when we don't want to be. Beautiful, enormous tomatoes can be purchased in your grocery store any time of the year, but they usually don't taste as good as I remember them tasting from my grandmother's garden.

So here's a crazy idea: What if it didn't have to be that way? What if technology got so good that it had no downside associated with it? Call me a dreamer, but I can see Casper smiling down on us all someday soon—lifesaving drugs without devastating side effects; automated financial services that maximize our portfolios without high fees or hours of work per month; ice cream that tastes better than ever, but has no fat or calories; even video games kids love to play but that also teach our children better than traditional means.

Within this concept of Casper technology, I know there is enormous opportunity. We are all waiting for technology to make us not only more efficient but also truly happier human beings. What a concept. If I wasn't so darn busy answering e-mails and cell phone calls, I'd probably look into it more.

Small Business Going Forward

It is admittedly difficult to make sweeping pronouncements about the future of small business in the United States. The prospects for a one-location retail video store versus a 90-person telemedicine delivery company are obviously not the same. However, there are a few macrochanges afoot that will affect us all in some way.

I recently attended a U.S. Chamber of Commerce small business summit. Hundreds of small business owners, policymakers, and politicians assembled to share information about the current state of small business in America. In a general session, a series of questions were asked of all attendees. These attendees punched answers into a keypad, and results of the questions posed were displayed on a giant screen in real time. The questions were topical, and the results were both interesting and surprising. The last question of the day, however, really spoke volumes: "What do you think should be the most important policy priority for small business?"

I've seen this question, or questions like it, asked of small business owners many times over the years. Not too long ago, the results would have been pretty spread out among a number of different issues, with tax and regulation burdens, access to capital, and tort reform leading the list. This time that didn't happen. Of the eight multiple-choice options given as possible answers, "reducing health care costs" was the answer for 68 percent of the attendees—over two-thirds! (In contrast, the combination of tax and regulatory burdens was only 6 percent.) In that answer lies the answer to a bigger question, "What is the future of small business in America?"

Small business success is, for the foreseeable future, going to increasingly revolve around people. Your inability to offer complete and competitive health care for your employees, relative to big business, is *the* limitation to growth for the near-term future. How long is near term? Until this situation is rectified, you can count on it being small business's number one nemesis.

I am optimistic that both sides of the political aisle will come together to help small business weather this storm. State and federal lawmakers understand the critical importance of this issue. I don't know exactly what type of plan they'll eventually devise, but it certainly will involve bundling our health care risks together through our local and national associations, chambers, or some yet-to-be-determined alliances. Keep your eyes on this major issue, and get involved if you can. Your representatives need to hear from people like you on this.

The long-term future of small business is also about people. For the rest of our lives, the rising demand for skilled, educated, and experienced employees will create brutal competition for the best and brightest. I anticipate middle-size and big business to throw money at this problem. That should not be your tactic, which brings me to my final macrochange.

THE PURSUIT OF PURPOSE

This entire book has tried to present a big picture, broad-strokes framework, with specific insights and suggestions for business owners like you. Now I'd like to end both this chapter and this book with a really big idea that I hope you can and will find useful.

I am seeing signs that this country, indeed Western civilization, is experiencing a fundamental shift. I suppose everyone living in a specific time at a specific place has a sense that things are happening around him or her that seem really important. It's possible that's happening to me. But I have been on this planet for well over 40 years, and I've never seen a more clear and broad-based shift in our perception of what it means to be alive. People in this country now have more materially than any other people have had in the history of mankind. Yet, here's the shift. It's not enough. For the first time ever, I believe we're starting to see that it will never be enough.

A lot of themes and ideas have been reiterated in this book. Here I'm going to leave you with one: The only way you can achieve sustainable growth is through truly outstanding people. Outstanding people are reassessing their lives, their priorities, and their purpose. A small business that consistently understands the workforce's newfound pursuit of purpose will have an enormous advantage over those who simply have more money.

I have laid out seven rules of small business growth. It starts with a company's sense of purpose, and it ends with that company's recognition of the importance of purpose in its people. Herein lies the future of your small, but soon to be growing, business.

SUGGESTED NEXT STEPS

1. Identify your key internal indicators of growth. Prepare a report on these keys to growth that you can review at least once a week.

2. Take the time to regularly consider both the major forces of change and potentially important weak signals affecting your industry. Your 50 magazines a month will be a very good start.

3. Before each growth planning session, find a way to rank the possible impacts of these major forces of change and weak signals. Be sure to consider how likely and how disruptive the change could be.

4. Keep a close eye on China over the next few years. Changes in China will impact your business in a big way someday soon.

5. Look for ongoing signs of change in the human condition and their ongoing pursuit of purpose. Find ways to connect those changes back to your organization's overall sense of purpose.

APPENDIX

PERSONALITY TESTS THAT MEASURE ENTREPRENEURIAL TYPES

MYERS-BRIGGS TYPE INDICATOR (MBTI)

In the early 1900s, the well-known psychologist Carl Jung developed a theory on personality typology. Katharine C. Briggs and Isabel Briggs Myers furthered Jung's theory on personality typologies and in 1962 developed the Myers-Briggs Type Indicator (MBTI) to examine the different personality types of people. In her book, *Introduction to Type: a Description of Theory and the Applications of the Briggs-Myers Type Indicator,* sixth edition (Center for Applications of Psychological Type, 1998), Isabel Myers-Briggs lists and explains the four categories of personality types:

1. *E/I: Extroversion versus Introversion* (where you focus your attention)
   E: Focus on the outer world and external environment
   I: Focus on the inner world

2. *S/N: Sensing versus Intuition* (how you acquire information)

   S: Finding things out through your senses; appreciating the realities of a situation

   N: Finding meanings, relationships, and the possibilities of things; looking at the big picture and essential patterns

3. *T/F: Thinking versus Feeling* (how you make decisions)

   T: Thinking logical consequences of any choice/action

   F: What is important to you or others; person-centered

4. *J/P: Judgment versus Perception* (how you orient toward the outer world)

   J: Judging attitude (thinking or feeling); likes to regulate and control life

   P: Perceptive process (sensing or intuition); flexibility; spontaneity

Where you fall on these four continuums leads to your preference for a particular personality trait. The various combinations of these four traits point to a total of 16 possible combinations. For instance, I am an ENFP (Extroverted, Intuitive, Feeling, Perceiver), often described as an "inspirer" or "persuader."

ENFPs are both "idea" people and "people" people, who see everyone and everything as part of a bigger whole. They want to both help and be liked and admired by other people. They are interested in new ideas in principle, but often discard many of them for one reason or another. ENFPs are also known for:

- Looking at information from a global viewpoint and spotting patterns and relationships that lead to an understanding of the key issues
- Focusing more on possibilities for the future than the here-and-now

- Enjoying change, challenge, and variety
- Being interested in evolutionary development, with an eye on the strategy
- Acting as a catalyst for change
- Contributing creative ideas, particularly those involving people
- Including others in the process of developing ideas and vision and being very accepting of contributions, even of varying quality
- Generating team spirit though the ENFP's own energy and enthusiasm

The potential ways in which an ENFP can drive people crazy include:

- Losing sight of the main purpose of the discussion and going off on tangents
- Initiating too many projects and not being able to deliver on all of them
- Talking too much
- Introducing too much change and not leaving well-established, workable routines alone
- Appearing to dominate in team efforts

I am an ENFP, no doubt about it. Ask people whom I've worked for or with, and they will tell you that the preceding description is very accurate. Ask my wife, and she'll tell you it's spooky how accurate it is.

The MBTI has been extensively used to evaluate personality types to help people choose careers to best suit their types. It is probably the best known and most widely used personality test. The MBTI also has been used with other tests to try to measure the predominant personality traits of successful entrepreneurs. Four of the most widely used tests that have been developed to help individuals evaluate their abilities to function as an entrepreneur are the Entrepreneurial Aptitude Test (EQ Test), the EQ Guide, the EQ Factor, and the Strong Interest Inventory.

The Entrepreneurial Aptitude Test (EQ Test)

Dr. Edward J. Fasiska and Deborah Gay Fasiska developed the EQ Test in the mid-1980s. In their book *The Fingerprints of the Entrepreneur,* revised edition (Pittsburgh, PA: Laserlight Publishers, 1987), they attempt to classify the personality traits of successful entrepreneurs, starting with the MBTI's four different personality preferences. According to the Fasiskas, extroversion and intuition are the key personality traits of the *classical entrepreneur.* Thinking rather than feeling is also an essential personality preference of entrepreneurs for them to plan, devise, and accomplish the necessary objectives that are needed to start their own businesses.

The EQ Test consists of 100 multiple-choice questions to distinguish what the authors define as the *classical entrepreneur* from the other personality types. They classify the ENTP type (with extroversion, intuition, thinking, and perceiving) as the ideal entrepreneur.

The EQ Test also assesses individuals for the following *operational traits:*

- *Idea attitude:* the ability to turn creative pursuits into a reality
- *Strategy attitude:* the ability to formulate a strategic plan to accomplish your goals
- *Planning attitude:* the ability to devise an operation to accomplish your objective

- *Implementation attitude:* the ability to follow through with projects

Outer PSE Adaptability, an individual's ability to work outside his or her own "personal sphere of equilibrium," is the third category in the EQ Test used to classify individuals in the EQ Inventory.

In the inventory, the possible scores for the *entrepreneurial success index* range from zero to 100. The average score is 56. According to the test, a person whose scores range between 65 and 100 is more likely to succeed compared to individuals whose scores fall below 65.

In *The Fingerprints of the Entrepreneur,* the Fasiskas describe the successful entrepreneur as someone who seeks autonomy, is flexible, deals well with confusion, is action oriented, and is somewhat of a risk-taker. They also say that it is easier for entrepreneurial types to come out of their own sphere and operate in the outer world. The authors list the three personality preferences for entrepreneurs with high success rates: extroversion, intuition, and perception.

The Fasiskas also compare entrepreneurs to other types of people who work for large companies. They describe executives in these companies as people who usually tend to be more rigid in their daily operations and have more difficulty switching gears. The entrepreneur, on the other hand, exhibits greater flexibility and shows more ease at adapting to new philosophies or ways of doing things.

The Entrepreneurial Quotient (EQ) Factor

The EQ Factor, a further study developed by Dr. Edward J. Fasiska while he was president of operations at the Carnegie Mellon Research Institute, was released in 1998. It is an extended version of the EQ Test and uses entrepreneurial profiling.

Focusing on personality traits and management styles, the EQ Factor was developed to help people choose an ideal career path based on their personal profile. It gives people the ability to compare their traits to the traits of successful entrepreneurs by allowing them to look not only at their thinking processes but also their operating processes. Referred to as the "IQ Test of Business," the test addresses entrepreneurial character traits while defining the strengths and limitations of a business.

The EQ Model (also called the EQ Guide)

After Edward J. Fasiska developed the EQ Test and EQ Factor, he continued to develop testing strategies to define the successful entrepreneurial type. In assessing the personality type of the successful entrepreneur, Wonderlic has added the MBPI and Fasiska's EQ model to its own test. In doing so, Wonderlic's test compares individuals taking the test to a database composed of 1,167 successful entrepreneurs and 1,118 successful corporate executives. It is a 100-item questionnaire composed of different sections and subsections with summary scales, their corresponding subscales, and ideal scores with each that measures the ideal entrepreneurial type. The summary scales and subscales are:

- *Adaptability*
- *Managerial Traits*
  —Risk Tolerance
  —Time Management
  —Creativity
  —Strategic Thinking
  —Planning
  —Goal-Orientation

- *Personality Traits*
  —Extroversion
  —Intuition
  —Thinking
  —Perceiving
- EQ Index

According to the EQ Model, the closer you score to the "ideal score," the greater your chances are to succeed as an entrepreneur.

BRIEF DESCRIPTION OF
THE SUMMARY SCALE

The *Adaptability Scale* measures your comfort level and ability to adjust to new or changed situations, new people, and new life experiences. The section on *Managerial Traits* measures your "entrepreneurial potential" in the following categories: risk tolerance, time management, creativity, strategic thinking, planning, and goal orientation. *Personality Traits* measures your entrepreneurial potential using the four personality-preference categories from the MBTI: Extroversion versus Introversion, Intuition versus Sensing, Thinking verses Feeling, and Perceiving versus Judging.

The *EQ Index* is a final summary scale composed of 16 EQ Managerial Types and the 16 MBTI personality types. In the subsection on *EQ Managerial Types,* the test lists 16 types of managers in two separate categories—*the creative managerial type* and *the traditional managerial type.* In both categories, there are eight managerial profiles listed based on the different kinds of managerial styles. In this section, the percentages of entrepreneurs and operations executives are listed for each type. The EQ Index also contains a subsection on *EQ Personality*

Types, listing the 16 traditional personality types from the MBTI. One-word character descriptions are listed for each personality type. For example, an ENTJ is referred to as a *commander.* Twenty-eight percent of the entrepreneurs in Wonderlic's database fall into this category. However, less than 1 percent are operations executives. The ESTJ personality type is labeled as the *implementer.* Twenty-nine percent of ESTJ individuals are entrepreneurs, while 8 percent are operations executives. According to the EQ Model, ENTJ *commanders* and ESTJ *implementers* are two of the MBTI personality types that are considered most likely to succeed as entrepreneurs compared to all of the other personality types.

The comprehensive EQ Model is designed to provide people with an increased understanding of their entrepreneurial strengths and weaknesses. The test assesses three different areas in the final *EQ Index: adaptability, managerial traits* and *personality traits.* Test takers are rated on a scale based on their conceived abilities to become successful entrepreneurs.

The Strong Interest and MBTI Inventory Type Indicator

The inventory provides general information about career interests and comparisons between the different types of occupations that are listed. Your results from the test will list possible career options for you, along with additional information about these options.

According to Allen L. Hammer's *Strong and MBTI Entrepreneurial Report,* when the Strong and MBTI inventories are used together, they can help you think about opening your own business by allowing you to do the following:

1. Compare your results from the inventory to the results of others with already-existing businesses.

2. Detail the tasks that are required for you to run a business, the role of your personality in doing these tasks, and then evaluate your personal interests.
3. Compare work, learning, leadership, and risk-taking styles with small business owners.

The Strong Interest Inventory measures your results with others who are already experienced in their careers. It also explores the similarities between your interests and the interests of others working in more than 100 specific occupations.

Strong's *General Occupational Themes* show six different types of people and their work environments:

- *Conventional (C):* accounting, processing data
- *Enterprising (E):* selling, managing
- *Artistic (A):* creating or enjoying art
- *Social (S):* helping, instructing
- *Realistic (R):* building, repairing
- *Investigative (I):* researching, analyzing

The report also characterizes the tasks involved in running a small business:

- Marketing and sales
- Financial management
- Operations and administration
- Human resources
- General management

It compares small business owners as they relate to these five tasks. It can compare your skills to others and show you how others operate and run their businesses. The report lists their working styles, learning environments, leadership styles, and risk-taking and adventure propensities. The test may help guide you to decide if you have the personality type or interests to open your own business.

OTHER SCHOLARLY STUDIES ON
ENTREPRENEURIAL SUCCESS
Crant (1996)

In his article, "The Proactive Personality Scale as a Predictor of Entrepreneurial Intentions" (Journal of Small Business Management, July 1996), J. Michael Crant considers factors of individual differences among entrepreneurs, while exploring their behavioral intentions. Based on other findings that used the Proactive Personality Scale at the time, Crant says that the entrepreneurial intentions of individuals seem to be closely related to gender, education, having an entrepreneurial parent, and possessing a proactive personality. A person with a *proactive personality* is an individual who is unconstrained in certain situations and affects environmental change, rather than allowing environmental change to affect him or her. Proactive personality types, he asserts, act on opportunities after identifying them. People in this category also take initiative and action with ease to create change. According to *interactionist theory,* Crant claims that proactive personality types may have the tendency to enter into entrepreneurial careers.

The concept of proactive personality was first developed in 1993. The Proactive Personality Scale uses a 17-item scale with questions that range from 1 ("I strongly agree") to 7 ("I strongly disagree"). Crant suggests that *the personality scale* may be used with other personality assessment tests to help you predict your predisposition to becoming an entrepreneur.

Byers, Kist, and Sutton (1997)

In their 1997 article, "Characteristics of the Entrepreneur: Social Creatures, Not Solo Heroes," Tom Byers, Helen Kist, and

Robert I. Sutton (CRC Press LLC, October 27, 1997) state that academic research places too much emphasis on personality traits to predict entrepreneurial success rates. Personality factors, they believe, do not provide a large enough explanation on the success and failure rates of entrepreneurs. They argue that personality and the demographic and social backgrounds of entrepreneurs hardly affect the success rates of entrepreneurs. Byers, Kist, and Sutton argue that the key characteristics (e.g., commitment, opportunity obsession, tolerance of risk, ambiguity and uncertainty, creativity, self-reliance, the ability to adapt, and the motivation to excel) that successful entrepreneurs have been labeled with in many studies can also be used to measure the success rates of individuals working in other fields. Not enough credit, they believe, has been given to other factors, such as opportunity, constraints, and other people's actions, when trying to distinguish the success rates among entrepreneurs.

In their research, Byers, Kist, and Sutton focus on the social implications of entrepreneurship rather than on their individual activities. According to them, leadership and its social role are key to understanding the nature of entrepreneurship. Social networks play an integral role, because they give entrepreneurs access to the resources they need to start a business. They believe more studies should focus on social factors, and fewer studies should study personality types when identifying the characteristics associated with their success rates.

Olson (2000)

In his article, "The Role of Entrepreneurial Personality Characteristics on Entry Decisions in a Simulated Market," David E. Olson (USASBE/SBIDA Annual National Conference, 2001) asserts that the characteristics used to define entrepreneurs "have often been confounded by questions of cause and effect, ambiguous definitions, and conflicting or inconclusive results." Instead, he uses a behavioral approach to study ambition, risk-taking, and locus of control (i.e., whether you believe that the outcomes of your actions are contingent on what you do or not) of entrepreneurs who are just entering the market. In the study, Olson uses an experimental game theory, in which his subjects are asked whether they would choose to enter simulated markets. He also gives them a questionnaire with subscale questions on ambition, risk-taking, and locus of control. In these three areas, based on his study, he has found no significant differences between entrepreneurs and the general public.

Baron and Markman (2000)

Robert A. Baron and Gideon D. Markman research the social skills of successful entrepreneurs and write about it in their article, "Beyond Social Capital: How Social Skills Can Enhance Entrepreneurs' Success" (*Academy of Management Executive*, vol. 14, 2000). While they do not discount the personality traits or cognitive skills of successful entrepreneurs, their primary focus lies in the specific social skills that enable some entrepreneurs to achieve success more easily than others, including:

- The ability to read others accurately
- The ability to make favorable first impressions
- The ability to adapt to a wide range of social situations and be persuasive

They also characterize situations where good social skills—the ability to gain a favorable reputation while building capital; any previous, relevant experience; and direct personal contacts that give the entrepreneur the access to venture capitalists, potential customers, and others—would allow some entrepreneurs to achieve a higher level of success over others. They assert that face-to-face interactions could strongly influence an entrepreneur's level of success.

Baron and Markman identify four social skills that they believe are crucial for entrepreneurs to develop:

- *Social perception:* Accurately perceiving others' motives, traits, and intentions
- *Impression management:* The proficiency to encourage positive reactions in others
- *Persuasion and influence:* The skills for changing the attitudes or behavior of others in desirable directions
- *Social adaptability:* The ability to adjust to a wide range of social situations and feel comfortable with individuals from diverse backgrounds

To illustrate the importance of these skills, Baron and Markman give instances in which they may be helpful. *Social perception skills* are valuable in cases where the individual would need to make presentations to investors and customers, attract and select partners and employees, and conduct negotiations. *Impression management skills* are useful in situations such as obtaining finances, attracting employees, and dealing with customers and suppliers. *Persuasion and social influence skills* are helpful when obtaining financing, recruiting employees, dealing with customers and suppliers, and conducting negotiations. *Social adaptability skills* are helpful when an individual is trying to establish business relationships with strangers (e.g., cold calls) or working with people from diverse backgrounds.

Similar research supports Baron and Markman's findings. For example, in one study it was found that entrepreneurs who communicate more frequently tend to become more successful than entrepreneurs who lack communication skills.

Social skills seem to play a large role for an entrepreneur to achieve success.

Korunka, Frank, Lueger, and Mugler (2003)

Christian Korunka, Hermann Frank, Manfred Lueger, and Josef Mugler highlight a study that they conducted in the fall of 2003 at Baylor University in their article, "The Entrepreneurial Personality in the Context of Resources, Environment, and the Start-Up Process" (*Entrepreneurship Theory and Practice*, vol. 28, no. 1, September 2003). They analyzed the personality characteristics of entrepreneurs in conjunction with personal resources, the environment, the start-up process, and the organizing activities of a newly formed business. In the study, they sampled 1,169 individuals who were in the beginning stages of business development. By comparing start-up business entrepreneurs to new business owner-managers, they found three different patterns of personality characteristics in entrepreneurs: a high need for achievement, a high internal locus of control (i.e., the outcomes of your actions are contingent on what you do), and medium risk-taking propensity. They claim that these characteristics confirm the "classic" personality traits associated with the successful entrepreneur. To a degree, they were able to define the entrepreneur's personality traits as they correlate to environmental factors, resources, and a start-up business's organizing activities.

INDEX